PN 4874 .P38

THE
DREW PEARSON
STORY

THE
DREW PEARSON
STORY

by

FRANK KLUCKHOHN

and

JAY FRANKLIN

CHAS. HALLBERG & COMPANY

Publishers

CHICAGO, ILLINOIS 60610

FRANK KLUCKHOHN

Frank Kluckhohn served twenty years as a correspondent for *The New York Times*. From 1929, to 1933, he was on the Washington, D. C., staff. His next big assignment was the Spanish Civil War. He was first to report the German intervention and also the first to interview General Francisco Franco. After an assignment in Mexico City, he authored the book, *The Mexican Challenge*. In 1938, he returned to the Washington staff and from 1939 to 1942 was White House correspondent.

Frank Kluckhohn went to war in 1942, covering London, North Africa and the Far East. In 1945, he was made Chief of the Pacific Bureau and was the first newspaper reporter to interview Hirohito. After the war, he became Chief of the Latin American Bureau.

Leaving *The New York Times* in 1948, he served as the titled *Advisor* to the first Secretary of Defense, James V. Forrestal and later as Special Assistant to the first four administrators of Security and Counsular Affairs in the Department of State.

In addition to his early book on Mexico, Frank Kluckhohn wrote the best sellers, *America, Listen* and *Lyndon's Legacy*, along with *The Naked Rise Of Communism* and *What's Wrong With U. S. Foreign Policy*.

JAY FRANKLIN

Jay Franklin is the familiar pen-name of John Franklin Carter who has operated behind the scenes of national politics for the last two generations. Like Mr. Kluckhohn, he is a graduate of *The New York Times*, where he was for many years the Senior Book Review Editor, and has seen diplomatic service in Rome, Constantinople, and the Department of State. He also served in the Department of Agriculture during the first New Deal and was in charge of Special White House Intelligence during World War II.

Jay Franklin has been writing books for four decades, starting with *Man Is War*. He is the author of some thirty books, both fiction and non-fiction, a number of which were published under various pen-names. He has written political speeches for Roosevelt, Truman, Dewey, and Nelson Rockefeller, among others. He also wrote a syndicated political column, "We, The People" for some twenty years and numerous magazine articles.

The writing of The Drew Pearson Story was a feat comparable to belling the cat. Perhaps others could have done it but Kluckhohn and Franklin did it. They alone have hereby demonstrated the ability and the courage to swat the political gadfly of our time.

TABLE OF CONTENTS

THE
DREW PEARSON
STORY

A City To Loot

Today Drew Pearson wields more power from Washington than all but two or three persons in Government. He is virtually a government within a government with his own corps of agents and informants reaching into every corner of the ever growing Federal establishment.

Through almost any means, he has held sway for three and a half decades and outlasted Kings, Presidents and Communist Party Chairmen, passing out some truth and a great deal of invention, all of it highly controversial. He is not tied down by the F.C.C. or by frightened network executives and he is, in fact, answerable to no one. He even bought the syndicate which distributes the newspaper part of his output.

The man himself is a colorful enigma, a showman with a snow-white mustache, a human cash-register entranced with the sound of dropping coins, a man willing to use under-the-table methods to get news but one who cannot forget he is a Quaker who recognizes social conscience. He is in one word — fascinating — whether you hate

1

him, despise him, abominate him, like him or admire him. For he is a unique phenomenon.

Back in the 1920's, when Washington's voice was beginning to change half-way between the squeaky treble of a small town and the resonant bass of a world-capital there were no syndicated national columnists apart from good old Mark Sullivan and the inevitable David Lawrence and there was no daily crisis for columnists to interpret or invent.

In those days, Drew Pearson was simply another Washington newspaperman, covering the State Department beat for the *Baltimore Sun* and doing it very well indeed — so well that the Department naively believed, perhaps prophetically, that he was already rifling confidential files and bribing clerks. The explanation for his insight into American foreign policy was simple. He cultivated the Latin American diplomats at a time when most of the Department's officials — except for a handful of Foreign Service officers like Jack Cabot and Norman Armour — considered them beyond the social pale and cultivated the Western Europeans instead. So the Latin diplomats told Pearson what was doing and he reported it, without attribution, and made his name feared and respected.

Otherwise, in those days the action was not in Washington at all, it was in Wall Street, Broadway and Hollywood. Men like Clarence Barron, Roger Babson and Professor Irving Fisher were the nation's pet pontificators; Cholly Knickerbocker, Walter Winchell and Hedda Hopper were developing the gossip column. Occasionally a writer like Frank Kent or Frank Simonds surfaced with a background article on national or international affairs; but, America paid more attention to channel swimer Gertrude Ederle and flyer Charles Lindbergh than to all the Washington correspondents laid end to end.

Forty years later, this changed. Drew Pearson succeeded in combining the racy half-truths and sly innuendoes of the Broadway gossip column with the crack-of-doom prognostications of a Nostradamus. He claimed to be syndicated by over 600 newspapers with 40,000,000 readers, although these figures were padded by a flock of small weeklies which used Pearson's clip-sheets as "filler-copy." In truth, there were barely 150 dailies that regularly subscribed to "The Washington Merry-Go-Round" with a total circulation of 10,000,000 readers. His weekly broadcasts, (despite a spotty record on his predictions) reached an additional 12,000,000 Americans over some 250 radio stations. With his words thus reaching some 22 million Americans, he was feared, courted, denounced and deferred to by the highest in the land.

Pearson had been called a liar by countless men in public life, including three Presidents of the United States. One of them (naturally it was Truman) even called him a son-of-a-bitch over a nation-wide radio broadcast. Pearson's aides have installed "bugs" in hotel bedrooms, ransacked Senatorial files and then in typical fashion hid behind a skirmish line of libel suits and lawyers. Pearson raised the power of the Fourth Estate to the level of a private empire with the cool audacity of a John D. Rockefeller putting together the Standard Oil Company, and the chromium-plated drive of a Jimmy Hoffa operating the Teamsters' Union. Pearson even chaperoned Chief Justice Earl Warren on a clandestine visit to Nikita

Khrushchev in the Crimea. All this at a time when
the press, as a whole, was steadily losing influence and the newspaper business was in a state
of economic decline.

Not since the "Junius Letters" turned British
politics into a shambles two hundred years ago
had there been anything to equal this one man
journalistic performance. It is still hard to believe
and, for many Washingtonians, increasingly hard
to take.

How did it happen? Upon what meat did this
Caesar feed that he became so monstrous? What
kind of ambition does it take to rise from the
hum-drum level of honest reporting in a Washington newspaper bureau to the colossus of syndicated
column-writing and national broadcasting?

What happened, basically, was that in those
forty years Washington changed, America changed,
the world changed and Pearson took advantage of
the mass media to twist its purpose to profitable
power.

The Wall Street stock market crash of October,
1929, was described at the time as an attempt to
give America back to the Indians, only to find that
the Indians didn't want it. The New Deal was sometimes jokingly interpreted as an attempt to put
the country back into shape so that next time the
noble Red Man would not refuse it as a gift. Wise-
cracks aside, the fact was that with the Panic
and the Great Depression there died one great
American dream: that Industry and Wall Street
would somehow make us all rich without our having
to work for it. In time, this tinsel vision was replaced by an equally pathetic belief: that government credit was a well that could never run dry
and that there was no human problem from can-

cer to incompetence which could not be solved
by a group of men meeting in an air-cooled chamber near the Potomac and solemnly intoning "seven
billion dollars" in faith that this incantation would
automatically create the wealth, labor, materials
and intelligence needed to handle the situation.

Long before this latter-day dream had begun to
turn into a nightmare, there was a fantastic
hypertrophy of syndicated Washington columnists,
so many of them that a large volume could — and
undoubtedly will — be written on the subject.
Where, in the 1920's, almost alone among American newspaper writers, Heywood Broun had cru-
saded for Sacco and Vanzetti right up to the electric chair, in the 1930's there were crusaders
everywhere and for every cause. After presiding
editorially over the liquidation of the famous old
New York World, Walter Lippmann moved to
Washington and began the interminable process of
solving, three times a week, in clear and logical
language, one or another of the problems which
had beset the human race for some 3,000 years —
in exactly 600 words — no more, no less — per
problem. Dorothy Thompson discovered — to quote
Sir Wilmot Lewis of the *London Times* — the
secret of perpetual emotion and Elmer Davis (no
columnist himself) announced when Hitler marched
into Poland, "Dorothy Thompson has been right all
the time and isn't it the hell of a world where
Dorothy Thompson is right:"

Joseph Alsop teamed up with Robert Kintner
and thrice a week shrilly discovered the obvious
before going off to Naval Intelligence, jumping
ship at Hong Kong and joining Clare Chennault's
Flying Tigers just in time to be interned by the
Japanese. Learning of this at the National Press

Club bar, the late C. P. "Peck" Trussey of Drew's old paper, the *Baltimore Sun,* reacted instantaneously. "If the Japs have Joe Alsop, it's their own goddamed fault," Peck snapped.

Marquis Childs started a long-drawn career of ladling out Socialism and branch water from coast to coast, in the artless belief that "the middle way" between Fascism and Communism would lead to Utopia instead of Armageddon. David Lawrence rigidly upheld the Conservative cause, somewhat handicapped by the fact that he still regarded himself as a Liberal. Mark Sullivan went bravely down the line for old-fashioned Teddy Roosevelt Progressivism. Yet on the whole the rat-pack of new columnists were well to the left of the old line of demarcation between reform and reaction in a changing society.

It was during this period that Drew Pearson and Bob Allen launched their "Washington Merry-Go-Round" column on the heels of their resounding anonymous book publishing success of the same title in 1931. Their book had been published anonymously, right enough, but not anonymously enough to protect them from the wrath of the White House. Both authors lost their newspaper jobs, by official request, in the depth of the Depression and were forced into the newspaper column writing game by economic necessity and a sure sense of opportunity.

When Marshall Bluecher first set eyes on London after the Battle of Waterloo, the old Prussian soldier exclaimed, "What a city to loot!" Under the New Deal, Washington was rapidly becoming a wonderful place to plunder, and the Pearson-Allen column with its adroit combination of keyhole gossip and an aching void in "inside" political and international reporting, was of all Washington columns far and away the best adapted for buccaneering.

It took the Second World War for this potential to be fully grasped and exploited. Bob Allen was a warm-hearted, generous and impulsive man, adjectives that have never been applied to his partner. As chief of the Washington bureau of the *Christian Science Monitor*, in addition to having a good nose for news and a talent for leg-work, Bob Allen also had a sense of professional responsibility for what he wrote. As long as he co-authored the column it was brilliant, colorful but dependable a good part of the time.

Drew Pearson was freed of this millstone when Allen was commissioned into the Army and went to war with General George Patton. In his absence, Drew Pearson euchred Allen out of his share of the column as deftly as, he had, ten years earlier, taken the wife of his *Baltimore Sun* colleague, George Abell. With Allen out of the way, Pearson went to town.

The necessary secrecy and censorship — voluntary and imposed — of war time provided a marvellous opportunity for invention. What Pearson pretended to do was to tell his public what really went on behind closed and guarded doors in the Pentagon, the White House, on Capitol Hill — whether it had or not. No official denial could be accepted because of war time secrecy and censorship, so "The Washington Merry-Go-Round" had a field day.

So long as Franklin Roosevelt lived, he had some control over Pearson's wilder impulses and on occasion leaked important news, such as Ambassador Billy Phillips' report on India, through

Pearson. With F.D.R.'s death, however, all bets were off and the column came into its own. For 20 years it has stuck to the simple formula of Danton: "Always Audacity!" To that Drew has added "For Profit!" Pearson follows the doctrine of attack and minimizes defense. When sued for libel Pearson fights back; even if he finally has to settle out of court, he prudently keeps the bulk of his multi-million-dollar fortune judgment-proof in his second wife's name.

Pearson has probably made more enemies, published more loose or unfounded charges, called more names, published more guesses and inventions, pursued more vendettas — up to and even beyond the grave — than any other man in journalistic history. Anyone with less self-confidence, cold gall and conviction that he is essentially right even when all his facts are wrong, would long since have been crushed beneath the weight of official hostility, editorial timidity and, at points, public indignation.

In the last analysis, it is the editors and publishers themselves who are responsible for this incredible performance. In the 1920's, during what has since been characterized as the Era of Wonderful Nonsense, the American newspapers virtually abdicated any real social criticism or sustained economic analysis. They served instead as a cheering section for the Bull Market. They danced to the piping of the bankers and brokers of Wall Street. When the market collapsed and the New Deal took over, they promptly became the "one-party press" of later years, with the owners opposed to, and their writers and readers enthusiastically in favor of, the moderately Big Government measures the Roosevelt Administration proposed as a cure for economic disaster.

In order to work both sides of the street, however, many American newspapers resorted to a
flock of syndicated columnists, whose views might
appease their readership without committing the
publisher to F.D.R.'s big spending, bureaucratic
controlled bundle of industrial and agrarian her-
esies. The publishers even printed disclaimers
asserting the views were "the columnist's own."
In time, with the organization of American Newspaper Guild, the editorial and reporting staffs also
became one-party affairs — blindly following the
line as laid down — while the publishers either
went along with or, in a few cases, continued to
cling wearily to the Conservative side of the fence.

By then, of course, Drew Pearson's column had
ceased to be simply another syndicated feature
which could be dropped at will. It had become an
institution. Its cancellation automatically evoked
threats and protests, some of them from powerful
public figures whom Pearson conscripted in a
manner sometimes not unlike that of the MVD or
the Gestapo. But the real objection to dropping the
"Merry-Go-Round" was that it deprived the readers of a habit-forming hallucinatory drug. As one
member of the National Press Club bitterly pointed
out at the time when Pearson began publishing
Senator Dodd's private correspondence, "When
Drew is dead wrong, there's always the outside
chance that he might be right, and when he seems
absolutely right, there's the strong possibility that
he's dead wrong." As a matter of fact, the Washington newspaper corps holds Pearson not in low
esteem but in no esteem at all, as a sloppy reporter and reckless writer who would rather be
read than dead, and much rather be dreaded than
right.

This is, in a minor key, the unregenerate sour grapes reaction of the average man to one who has made a roaring financial and professional success of what has been described as journalistic garbage collection. Partly it is an instinctive recognition of the fact that Pearson is an institution apart from, and not a member of, the working news media. He belongs not in the class of Arthur Brisbane or even William Randolph Hearst. He is almost a government in his own right, conducting foreign policy and domestic affairs on the classical principles laid down by Niccolo Machiavelli and Nicolai Lenin. He is much more like Cesare Borgia than Emile Zola, closer to Stalin than to Tom Paine. Proclaiming that he serves the public by uncovering official hanky-panky, he has for years been a hatchet-man for special interests running the gamut from labor unions which long subsidized his broadcasts to Lyndon Johnson who, for a time bought him off.

Never in all human history has a single journalist commanded such influence, power and practical immunity from the laws which control ordinary reporters and which supposedly protect people from blackmail. And there are some men in American public life who are grimly determined that never again shall this be allowed to happen and many more who are afraid to let their similar sentiment be publicly known.

Pearson has come so far and developed such momentum that the real question is: For God's sake, how long will this fantastic performance go on and when will it stop? Or will it stop, now that he is coddling an heir apparent who is probably more Pearson-like than Drew himself, but not so adroit? This you will see as the show develops.

The Making Of A Columnist

No stars fell on Evanston, Illinois, on the night of December 13, 1897, when their first son was born to Paul Martin Pearson and his wife, Edna. Despite the fact that later victims of his pen and voice held that Andrew Russell Pearson was born with a cloven hoof in his mouth, there was little in the first thirty-odd years of Drew's life to indicate that this child of Quaker parents was destined to shake, or shake down, the American world into which he was born on the eve of the Spanish-American War and the era of progressive reform which thereafter dawned with Teddy Roosevelt.

There are Quakers and Quakers. Often they are saints. Sometimes they tend to exalt stubbornness and self-righteousness to major Christian virtues. Not infrequently they develop a prehensile instinct for money making that would be envied by a Hindu loan shark and make old Shylock look like a kindly philanthropist. The father, Paul Pearson, was a friendly, twinkling extrovert, a college professor

11

and Chautauqua lecturer who rose to be President
of Swarthmore, a Quaker College at Swarthmore,
Pennsylvania, and still later he was named Governor of the Virgin Islands, by Herbert Hoover,
apparently in the naive belief that this would serve
as a lightning-rod against his journalistic, eldest
son. Drew's mother, according to those who knew
her, made it easy to understand why the New
England Puritans whipped, branded and occasionally hanged "the Quiet People." Her saintly virtues had soured her. Be it said at once that Drew
did not take after his father, though his younger
brother Leon inherited some of the latter's sim-
plicity of heart and burbling friendliness.

Drew was above average in intelligence, born on
the right side of the tracks into a society which
was still fiercely individualistic and highly com-
petitive and which regarded the amassment of
material wealth as proof of virtue. He attended
Phillips Academy at Exeter, New Hampshire, under
the headmastership of the genial and tolerant
Lewis Perry. During summer vacations, Drew
accompanied his father on Chautauqua tours and
thus got a worm's eye view of America at a time
when his schoolmates were thinking in terms of
girls, tennis and swimming. The only incident of
note on the lecture circuit occurred in July, 1914;
he was arrested by Southern Railway police in a
small Georgia town for the crime of looking for
a water tap in the railway yards on a hot night in
the company of a small Negro boy. The case was
dismissed when he was brought before a magis-
trate the next morning.

In 1915, young Pearson matriculated at Swarthmore, where his father was then President, and
received his B.A. degree in June of 1919, that first

of the feverish post-war years which proved that the country into which he had been born had changed beyond belief. He did quite well at such minor athletics as swimming and he made Phi Beta Kappa, then, as now, the mark of real scholastic attainment. Armistice Day and Drew's 21st birthday came fairly close together and a few days before the end of World War I he enlisted in the U.S. Army and was promptly ordered to complete his college course.

His mother-in-law, Eleanor "Cissy" Patterson, later accused him of having "thee'd and thou'd" his way to stay out of the war but she was a fierce female when angry, and when she said this, she was very angry at Drew. As a Quaker, Drew can be assumed to have been a pacifist; his enlistment provided a practical way of completing his education at government expense, and few of the American college class of 1919, apart from naval aviators and graduates of Plattsburg, saw action in the war to "make the world safe for democracy." While it is understandable that Mrs. Patterson might well have wished Drew to die a hero's death before he married her only daughter, still the last thing he would have done was oblige her. As it happened, Drew did wear the uniform of the U.S. Army during his senior year at Swarthmore and is, presumably, entitled to be buried in Arlington National Cemetery. Extreme doubt exists as to whether any eternal flame will be lighted for him — at least there.

The next five years of Drew's life were the usual unedifying, aimless struggle of a young American on the make trying to wend his way in a strange world. He worked in a circus but not as an acrobat or clown. It is uncharitable but more accurate to suggest that he followed the elephants with a shovel and broom. He then shipped as a sailor to the Far East. He traveled by whatever means available and saw as much of the world as he could as quickly as he was able.

From 1919 to 1921, he made his first mark, starting out with a bang as Director of the American Friends Service Committee in Serbia, Montenegro and Albania. There he did not face bullets but he did face typhus and Balkan cooking, where even a boiled egg often tastes of goat. Next he lectured for a year as instructor in industrial geography at the University of Pennsylvania, also serving a number of stints as a Chautauqua lecturer about the United States, and in Australia and New Zealand.

Much as it would surprise his fellow-newspapermen, he started out on a program of realistic reporting and unusual enterprise. Jack Alexander, a good newspaperman himself, had this to say for Drew's debut in journalism:

The Washington Disarmament Conference came along in 1922, and with it a chance to rub elbows with the world's leading striped-pants wearers. Pearson enterprisingly manufactured the chance himself. He paid a visit to the editor of the Swarthmore student weekly, the *Phoenix,* of which he had once been editor himself, and suggested that his successor write to Secretary of State Hughes asking that Pearson be allowed to interpret the conference for college men. While in college, Pearson had founded something called the Intercollegiate Press Association and, at his urging, the letter was typed on one of the association's letterheads. Hughes thought the idea a good one, and Pearson got to attend the conference as correspondent for the Swarthmore *Phoenix* and the college-press association. After this coup, he was discussed on the Swarthmore campus, near which he lived, as one of the alumni most likely to succeed.

Soon afterward, Pearson transformed himself into a world

traveler. The transformation was accomplished with surprising rapidity. A world-traveler friend of his, who had had some success as a lecturer, lent him a copy of his publicity circular and, with his permission, Pearson converted the text to his own use, largely by substituting his own name for that of his friend. Marked "Confidential — Not For Publication," the circular, under the headline AROUND THE WORLD WITH DREW PEARSON, stated in part: "Asia, Africa and Europe are familiar fields to Drew Pearson. He has visited all three continents. He has an international point of view. . . As a lecturer on international politics, Pearson is known over most of this country and in England." It went on to describe the mysterious, teeming Orient, which Pearson now proposed to probe into, travelling by steamship, airplane, ox cart, automobile, on camel, on horse and on foot."

Instead of mailing the circular to newspaper editors, as a less imaginative young man might have done, Pearson took it to them personally, traversing the continent in day coaches, with stop-overs. Through fast talking, he sold thirty-five editors between Philadelphia and Seattle on the notion of buying dispatches which he proposed to mail back. In Seattle, from which he intended to work his way across the Pacific, his resourcefulness showed itself again. Turned down by the hiring halls because he lacked experience as a seaman, Pearson had his chest tattooed with a Turkish star and crescent, and haunted the halls once more with his shirt front unbuttoned. The ruse worked, and he shipped aboard a passenger vessel as an ordinary seaman, jumping ship at Yokohama.

His travels carried him through the Japanese islands and into Siberia, then down to Australia, where, in addition to sending home his regular dispatches, he made money by lecturing on the Japanese menace, which has always worried the Australians. From Australia, he sailed to India to interview Mahatma Gandhi. Unfortunately, Gandhi was in jail and couldn't be seen. On returning to the United States, Pearson made capital of him anyway; he interviewed Henry Ford, who had Gandhi-like ideas about decentralizing industry, and sold an article on the two decentralizers to the magazine *Asia*. Two years later Pearson went back to India to have another go at the Mahatma. This time the holy man was on a fast and couldn't be bothered, and to this day Pearson has never seen him.

In 1924, he held a job as lecturer on commercial geography at Columbia University; 1925 found him reporting on anti-foreign strikes in China. In mellow retrospect, these activities may be twisted into a professional pattern, but at the time he was a rolling stone who acquired little usable polish.

But oodles, oceans and seas of beautiful green moss came. In 1925, Drew made his first ten-strike. This naturally was not journalistic: it was matrimonial. It had long been an Ivy League axiom that it is just as easy to marry a rich girl as a poor girl. Drew was one of the few who not only did so but avoided paying the usual price of life-long subservience to the connubial purse-strings. His choice fell like a headsman's axe on Felicia Gizycka, only daughter of Cissy Patterson, publicized heiress of the McCormick and Patterson families. He met and courted Felicia at Mrs. Patterson's Wyoming ranch. He finally found and married her when she was slinging hash at a San Diego waterfront eatery to which she had fled to escape from her domineering mother and Drew. The couple had one daughter, baptized Ellen Cameron. "Cissy" gave her grandchild an elegant 285-acre Maryland farm as a present, but in due time Drew contrived to get personal possession of the $1,000,000 estate. He has retained it to this day in his second wife's name.

There is no purpose at this particular point of giving a blow-by-blow account of Cissy's resounding feud with her son-in-law. Mrs. Patterson was a law unto herself, clever, rich, and used to having her own way always and everywhere. Drew was not rich but wanted to be; he used her faults to work her like a garden patch for years. His marriage into the Patterson millions, however brief its duration, automatically put him on the king-row of social Washington. He gave up his nebulous New York job and moved into the egg-head ghetto of Georgetown in Washington. His new profession as a journalist, i.e., a newspaperman who carries a cane, also put him in a position to capitalize fully on his social and political connections. He reported the abortive Geneva Naval Conference of 1927 for the Consolidated Press; he was a member of the staff of David Lawrence's *United States Daily* from 1926 for six years; and in 1929 he also joined the Washington bureau of the *Baltimore Sun,* where he served as State Department correspondent for the next three years.

In short, ten years after he had received his sheepskin at Swarthmore, Drew Pearson had arrived as a top-rank Washington correspondent after a preparation which stood comparison with that of his competitors. Except for the fortune-hunting aspects of his courtship, marriage and speedy divorce from Felicia Gizycka, there was nothing of which he might need to be ashamed. All doors were opened to Mrs. Patterson's son-in-law. He was well-informed and fearless. In fact, when Hoover sent Drew's father down to the Governor's Palace at St. Thomas in the Virgins, the son's news-stories and commentaries were just as critical of Governor Pearson as of any other Hoover appointee. The world might not have been Drew's oyster but at least it was his cherry-stone clam. He was already to apply the tabasco sauce when the Stock Market blew up and the nation found itself kneedeep in depression before you could say "Andrew Mellon."

Leaders of both political parties and the entire financial and industrial community had contributed to this economic catastrophe. However, the Republicans were in power and they were held responsible. The Hoover Administration, as the "In's", was fair game for criticism, much of it deeply bitter, as unemployment mounted, prices and wages plummeted, and bankruptcies, failures, foreclosures and suicides multiplied. The entire economy ground toward a halt. It was at this precise moment, in 1931, that Drew Pearson and Bob Allen published their trail-blazing, anonymous potpourri about the scene in the Nation's Capitol. Entitled *Washington Merry-Go-Round*, it was one of the few books of the time which, if it did not make history, suggested that history was about to be made.

Thirty-five years later, the book is chiefly instructive as showing how angry otherwise intelligent members of the public can become when they discover that they have made fools of themselves. Later on, after Drew had appropriated their joint column while Bob Allen was off to war and had begun swinging the hatchet for various causes but always for his own power and profit, it was customary to credit Allen with the good reporting in *Washington Merry-Go-Round* and to blame the excesses and basic political illiteracy of its chit-chat on Drew Pearson. This formula does not entirely stand analysis.

Pearson's chapters on Secretary of State Henry L. Stimson, the State Department, the diplomatic corps (with one significant exception) and social Washington are not unreasonable, if irreverent. Some of Allen's Capitol Hill material, on the other hand, is depressingly partial and deeply biased. Both suffered from a "good guys" and "bad guys" complex, the People vs. the Interests and sentimental clap-trap. Both had their myopic eyes riveted on Washington and couldn't see the national forest for the District of Columbia trees. Neither of them offered a clue as to what might lie in store for the nation and the world. They drove full-speed ahead, but their vision was glued to the rear-view mirror and they could only see where they thought the nation had been and not where it was going.

On the whole, however, the *Washington Merry-Go-Round* was racy, informative, colorful, and evidenced a dawning talent for pinning labels and coining epithets that stuck. Henry L. Stimson became "Wrong Horse Harry," and the House of Representatives became "The Monkey House." It was the first to speak of a "brain trust." The Supreme Court, which was destined to be the focal point of national affairs for the next forty years, did not rate separate treatment; the greatest flattery was heaped upon the handful of Progressive Senators who were known collectively as "The Sons of the Wild Jackass." This illuminates the authors' political immaturity. The Senate, with the decay of States Rights, had already become the "rotten borough" branch of Congress. Its members from the underpopulated wide open spaces shone with a certain brilliance but often it was the brilliance of a dead mackerel in the moonlight. By contrast, the authors had no patience with the duly elected representatives of the American people in the House: then as now a hard-working, undramatic body of men who have to run for office every two years, who represent people, not sheep, trees or scenery, and who win, or lose office entirely on the basis of whether they serve the interests and convictions of their constituents, the People.

The only place where the book scored as per-
ceptive political reportage, was in its recognition
of the fact that the Washington newspaper corps
had become a Fourth Branch of government. A
certain retrospective humor attaches to their vir-
tuous assertion that Washington correspondents
"write not what they know but what the viciously
partisan and reactionary policy of their employer
dictates." In an apparent attempt to conceal their
authorship, Pearson and Allen included themselves
in their discussion of the press.

Bob Allen referred to himself, briefly and ob-
jectively, as "the youngest large bureau chief in
the capital" with "important newspaper experience
in the United States and abroad."

Later Drew Pearson came to write of Drew
Pearson: what an eloquent and inspiring theme!

Not since that amiable Christopher Morley, as
editor of the American edition of *Bartlett's Familiar Quotations*, gave himself twice as much space
as he accorded to Christopher Marlowe, one of
England's greatest poets, has there been anything
so self-revealing. Revealing also, amid the shower
of Irish confetti, was a highly laudatory chapter
on Carlos Davila of Chile. There were those who
suspected that Drew must have been deeply in-
debted to Davila.

At the time, *Washington Merry-Go-Round* was a
national smash hit. The authors imprudently followed it up with *More Merry-Go-Round*, more of a
gossip-mongering tittle-tattle than the first book.
And this time the pudding hit the fan. President
Hoover was facing a national election and did not
yet realize that his chance of reelection was the
chance of a snowflake at the equator. Although he,
like Pearson, had firsthand experience of China

and was a Quaker, he had not learned that one of the supreme offenses in Chinese society was to break another man's rice-bowl. Pearson never did learn this.

The Secret Service swiftly ferreted out the identity of the authors and the White House telephoned the publishers of the *Baltimore Sun* and the *Christian Science Monitor*. Both Bob Allen and Drew Pearson were summarily fired from their jobs. To paraphrase Edna Millay's comment in one of her sardonic little "Figs From Thistles" verses, they soon found that they had been locked into more than they had been locked out of. They were, in fact catapulted into writing the Washington Merry-Go-Round column — seven days a week. It was an immediate gold mine which is still giving up its valuable metal over a generation later.

The Merry-Go-Round

If you devoutly believe that riches constitute proof of divine favor, it follows that any means of acquiring wealth is pleasing to God. It also follows that any individual or group that stands in the way of your personal advantage or refuses to enhance your influence or power is an enemy of God. Against such evil, of course, all measures are justified. While the ideal of holy poverty, humility and self-effacing service permeates Catholicism, Islam and the great religions of India, it has a low rank in the Protestant ethic, not least among the Quakers.

To raise a daily newspaper column from the level of an honest trade to a major racket called for more than ordinary dedication. Among other things, it entailed kicking away the ladder on which Pearson mounted to success and discarding those who had helped him rise. In his ascent to his selected throne, Drew was compelled by his inner light to betray his patroness, his partner, his closest friend and even his own daughter.

It was, of course, Eleanor "Cissy" Patterson who gave him his head-start on this climb, via her daughter Felicia. You can judge a man of the world by the woman he marries, a gentleman by the way he treats his wife. After five years of marriage to Drew, Felicia became for a time an alcoholic and got a divorce, leaving her daughter Ellen in Drew's custody. This had the incidental advantage of enabling him to retain a biological pipeline to the Patterson millions. For reasons which might interest a psychiatrist, the divorce did not antagonize his former mother-in-law, Cissy Patterson, who, in 1930, had wheedled William Randolph Hearst into letting her publish the Washington *Times-Herald*. Between her tempestuous personality and her money she made a fantastic success of the newspaper and, when the Depression had eroded Hearst's gargantuan fortune, she bought the paper outright. For more than a decade, Cissy alternately petted and clawed at her former son-in-law, but she found the Washington Merry-Go-Round column a good investment even after she had indignantly relegated it to the funny-pages after one of her anti-Drew tantrums.

In those parts of *More Merry-Go-Round* which Drew had written, he had more than hinted that various male guests at Cissy's DuPont Circle mansion were not hunting for Easter eggs when they mounted to the bedroom floor. This breach of ordinary human decency, and ingratitude, not to mention the fact he had been a guest, roused Cissy Patterson to a white fury and only Arthur Brisbane's timely intervention prevented a major eruption on the front page of her newspaper. Later, when Cissy succeeded in having the worst of these

passages deleted from later editions of *More
Merry-Go-Round*, she calmed down and continued
her curious love-hate relationship with the man
who was divorced from her daughter.

After World War II opened just 25 years after
the fatal August of 1914, which dealt a death-blow
to European world-primacy, her antagonism extended to matters of Drew's political policy. She
was an isolationist, his column was interven-
tionist; she admired General Douglas MacArthur,
his column emphatically did not; by early 1942,
Cissy branded Pearson and Allen "the Headache
Boys" and accused them, in a front-page signed
editorial of having "over a period of years . . . by
false and sneering innuendo, attempted to smear
the reputation of a great man." Since by this time
Allen had gone off to war, the attack was really
against Drew.

She also publicly apologized for a Merry-Go-
Round attack on Secretary of Commerce Jesse
Jones, the salty Texan who had headed the Recon-
struction Finance Corporation and who had sar-
donically suggested that every dollar bill ought to
be stamped across the back "Return to New York
City."

It is probable that if Cissy Patterson had not
been so fabulously rich her erratic behavior would
not have been tolerated, but she was the last of the
dwindling herd of American multimillionaires who
were allowed privileges which would have sent
lesser people to jail or a mental hospital. However,
she dearly loved her grand-daughter, Ellen, and on
the child's tenth birthday presented her with a
285-acre farm on the Potomac, near Rockville,
Maryland, with Drew Pearson, the child's father
and legal guardian, being named trustee for the

estate.

That little caper was worth about $900,000 to Drew. Ten years later, Cissy discovered that Drew, as Ellen's father, had managed to persuade Drew, as Ellen's trustee, to sell himself the estate for $100,000, although Cissy Patterson was willing to pay three times as much to keep it out of Drew's hands. Since Ellen was a minor, Cissy took the case to court and Drew returned the valuable trust property to his daughter. However, Cissy was dead when Ellen came of age, and the daughter easily yielded to her father's persuasion and let him complete the deal for the original $100,000. Today it is worth $1,000,000 (according to Senator Dodd's libel suit against Pearson) but it is in Drew's second wife's name so that it is doubtful that it could ever be attached.

Now is not the place to record how Drew, after writing gleefully of the sexy antics of his mother-in-law and other Washington socialites, took the wife of his best friend and eventually — in 1936 — married her — a marriage which, incidentally, has lasted ever since. It would be unkind to suggest that he could not afford to divorce the receiver of all his property. It is, however, a legitimate comment that, following this exceedingly messy sex situation, Drew has drawn the line at publicizing sex-scandals in his column. It is a salutary rule that people who live in glass houses shouldn't throw stones.

Cissy's vituperation continued unchecked right up to the end of her publishing career. In one editorial, addressed to the G. I. Joes, she called Drew a "phony Quaker" and "a yellow-bellied slacker." In another full-page article, she compared him to Robespierre in the French Revolution — to the latter's advantage — and teamed him up with some of her other pet hates, Henry Wallace ("Crystal-Gazing Crackpot") and Walter Winchell ("Middle-Aged Chorus Boy"). Another attack was headlined "Quaker Oat Turned Into Sour Mash" and referred to Drew as "the weirdest specimen of humanity since Nemo, the Turtle-Boy." To George Abell, whose wife Luvie became the second Mrs. Pearson, Cissy once remarked that it was a pity they weren't in Chicago, because "there I could have Drew 'rubbed out.'"

The final outburst of Cissy's vehemence followed the transfer of the "Washington Merry-Go-Round" column from her Washington *Times-Herald* to Eugene Meyer's *Washington Post*. She complained that she had been double-crossed and mourned the column's lost circulation even as she had attacked its authors.

This brings up Pearson's second great betrayal — the long-drawn series of events, decisions and deceptions by which he appropriated the jointly owned column from his partner, Bob Allen.

There was once a famous drawing in *Punch* of the man who had managed to lose a bass-drum. Well, Drew is the only man in history who has managed to pocket a merry-go-round. The saga is worthy of an Al Capone. It recalls the legend of the Arab who, incautiously, let the camel put his nose under the tent only to find out that the whole camel followed and that there was no longer any room for him in his own tent.

In early 1930, Robert S. Allen, then head of the Washington Bureau of the *Christian Science Monitor*, began writing vivid articles debunking Washington for H. L. Mencken's *American Mercury*. Mencken suggested to Bob that he write a book

about Washington along the same lines. Allen needed
assistance in covering what passed for Washington
high society as well as the State Department; so
he asked Drew Pearson to write these chapters.
Nevertheless, the title "Washington Merry-Go-
Round" was Bob's and Bob wrote four-fifths of the
book himself. As already described, this led to
another book and to resounding journalistic success. The two writers co-authored other books,
including *Nine Old Men* — a belated assessment of
the Supreme Court's role in the political hay —but,
with characteristic magnanimity, Drew Pearson
fails in his self-written biography in *Who's Who* to
give Allen any credit for their books or for the
column itself, which Bob originally suggested.

During the 1930's, with Bob to do the leg-work
and provide both established facts and a measure
of restraint, Drew's talent for mischief-making,
scandal-mongering and slanted propaganda served
chiefly to add spice to a well-written, stimulating
and informative political gossip-column. By and
large at the start, it supported the Roosevelt policies — less critically than Fulton Lewis, Jr. and
John O'Donnell, but more so than Ernest Lindley
or Jay Franklin, who, having served as volunteer
John the Baptists for the coming of the New Deal
were emotionally committed to 100 per cent defense of its measures.

The "Washington Merry-Go-Round" went along
with the Administration but operated on the old
newspaper principle that "names make news" and,
instead of think-pieces á la Lippmann, produced a
sort of factual chatter that spread truth, as well
as suspicion and confusion, on a national scene
which was subject to any and every interpretation,
depending entirely on where you happened to sit.

This condition continued right up to the day when Bob Allen went off to war. Early in 1941, when Cissy Patterson was staging one of her anti-Drew tantrums and was editing the column, Bob, being caught in the middle, got tired of it all. He tipped off Eugene Meyer at the *Washington Post* that the column's contract with the *Times-Herald* was coming up for renewal and that unless Cissy announced her intention to renew the contract at least 30 days before it expired, the syndicate could make a deal with the *Washington Post*. Cissy forgot to write the letter, Meyer nipped in and bought the column for $100 a week. In those days, $100 a week for a syndicate feature was not to be sneezed at and was considerably more than she had been paying. Cissy Patterson hit the roof and figuratively at least, went on through it. It was too late. The column moved over to the *Washington Post* and has remained there ever since: in time, Cissy's entire paper followed its example and was engulfed and extinguished by the publication she had fought so long.

The column switch occurred in 1941. Hitler's war of conquest was off to a flying start; Poland and France had fallen, England had barely survived the Blitz, and Roosevelt had been reelected to a third term. It was as plain as an alderman's wife that America would soon come into the war with both feet; so Bob decided to enter the Army. He made a verbal deal, as between two honest newspapermen who had worked together for over ten years, that during his absence in the armed forces, ten per cent of the column's gross earnings should go for his interest in the feature, with Drew taking 90 per cent. Then just as he was about to step on the train in Washington's Union Station

to depart for basic training, Drew dashed up and
said that the 10 per cent arrangement wasn't altogether satisfactory to him, that there would be
expenses, etc. At that point the train pulled out.

In subsequent correspondence, Bob held out for
his right to the agreed-on 10 per cent, to be paid
by the syndicate; Drew suggested, instead, that he
would pay 10 per cent of the net earnings — allow-
ing for "expenses" — directly into Bob's account.
Bob forbade his bank to accept any direct deposits
from Drew in order not to compromise the original agreement. As a matter of fact, Drew Pearson
did not pay Bob one dime for the column for the
next two and a half years and then only disgorged
a few payments after Bob's wife, newspaperwoman
Ruth Finney, took legal action. In any case, Drew
never gave Bob an accounting for the column's
earnings — Drew wrote him "poor-mouth" letters
at the very time he was building a $100,000 air-
cooled mansion on his daughter's ex-farm, and
there is no knowing how much of Bob's share was
paid over to him.

This was because Bob lost his right arm in combat while serving with George Patton's armored
columns in the great sweep through southern Germany, and returned home, not only in great pain
but in a state of psychic shock in which he imagined
that his writing days were over. He also found the
column so encrusted, pitted and riddled with Drew's
feuds and vendettas that he hardly recognized it
and did not care to have his name associated with
this monstrous change-over from spirited political
reporting to irresponsible political power.

Allen perhaps should have sued, in law and in
equity, but he didn't. The camel kept the tent,
leaving the Arab in the cold. Thus the last chance

that Drew Pearson could be brought back into bounds was lost along with Bob's shattered arm and Pearson's broken word. In time, Bob Allen recovered his courage and bounce and resumed column-writing on his own: he had lost his right arm, but had saved his journalistic soul. Drew had lost nothing he valued — just honor.

The world was at his feet and, after Roosevelt's death, the only restraint upon him was his own conscience. That exerted the same restraint as gasoline upon a warehouse fire. What had happened to him during the war made it clear that Drew's future would be even more incendiary than his past.

High-Level Hatchet-Man

During World War II, Drew Pearson had been painfully loyal to the Roosevelt Administration. This was not only a record but was also because he claimed a great personal admiration for FDR. As will be made plain in the next chapter, it may have been more because he preferred to stay out of jail. What may be condoned as journalistic enterprise in time of peace comes close to treason when there is a war on, and, as will be developed in another context, after Pearl Harbor, in grabbing for the brass ring, the author of the "Merry-Go-Round" column snatched a large spray of poison ivy.

His reward for involuntary cooperation with the war-effort was to be made the beneficiary of repeated "leaks" from the very highest level of government, subject to an Administration ban against betraying the source and at the risk of formal official denial. This is heady stuff for any newspaperman; one of the inevitable results of Roose-

velt's cat-and-mouse game with the columnist was
to encourage Pearson in the belief after FDR's
death that he was above the law and answerable to
no one but himself. It enabled him to pursue his
personal vendettas under the guise of clobbering
FDR's enemies.

During the war, for instance, Pearson's repeated
abuse of General Douglas MacArthur (who once
sued Pearson but made the mistake of making an
out-of-court settlement) fitted neatly into Roosevelt's fear of MacArthur's possible political com-
petition. The New Deal Liberals had long held a
grudge against MacArthur because he obeyed President Hoover's order to evict the bonus marchers
from Washington. Had the General mutinied and
refused to obey the order, these same critics
would have blamed him for the consequences.

In any case MacArthur's public personality lent
itself to caricature. In private, he was a quiet,
attractive and brilliant gentleman. In public, he
was a showman — his enemies contended — over-
decorated and unsubtle.

More, FDR had several bones to pick with the
General. Roosevelt was intensely pro-Navy. Mac-
Arthur was not and, moreover, from Bataan he kept
calling for the Navy to come to the rescue of his
beleaguered troops. Worse still, Roosevelt was
afraid the GOP might nominate General MacArthur
for the Presidency in 1944, perhaps on the issue
of whether the war effort should concentrate in the
Pacific against Japan instead of in Europe against
Germany. So Drew Pearson, acting as hatchet-man
for FDR, went after General Douglas MacArthur.

He was also acting as a hatchet-man in Under-
secretary of State Sumner Welles' campaign against
his boss, Secretary of State Cordell Hull. FDR had

found "Judge" Cordell Hull difficult to manage.
Hull, a handsome Tennessean who had only one
idea — trade agreements — had been given the top
Cabinet job of Secretary of State to appease both
the Congress and the Southern wing of the Democratic Party. FDR intended to be his own Secretary
of State and was irritated by those diplomatic officials who would not play his game.

Hull easily knocked off Roosevelt's top brain-
truster, Professor Raymond E. Moley, after the
London Economic Conference of 1933, but Sumner
Welles was far more adroit and formidable. Like
FDR, Welles was a Groton-Harvard product and
had been a page at Roosevelt's marriage to his
cousin, Eleanor. Moreover, Hull was seriously ill
and absent from his post for many months during
the critical period of the war; so Welles, as Acting Secretary of State, not inhumanly aspired to
the top position. He hobnobbed repeatedly with
Drew and fed him material to be used in his rivalry with Secretary Hull.

The counter-attack was inevitable, vicious and
successful. There was much gossip to the effect
that Welles was a homosexual, a favorite British
intelligence gambit in putting pressure on the
American Government, but FDR's attitude was like
Lincoln's on the subject of Grant's addiction to
whiskey. Finally, in the summer of 1943, the issue
was brought to public light and Welles resigned.
He was an able diplomatic negotiator who had
earned the respect and resentment of the British
Foreign Office by standing up against Downing
Street's perennial attempt to do our political thinking for us. Here, too, however Drew had been on
safe ground in backing Roosevelt's friend.

The real pay-off came in 1944. FDR was getting

burned up by Churchill's influence in American domestic affairs. In addition to Sumner Welles' ouster, he blamed Churchill for Senate rejection of Bronx Boss Ed Flynn as Ambassador to Australia and, finally, Churchill had "ordered" him not to renominate pro-communist Henry Wallace as his running-mate in the 1944 camapign. Although Roosevelt was annoyed with Wallace for having walked off with the Administration's left-wing labor support, he did not relish taking orders from anyone, least of all from Churchill. So he sent Ambassador William Phillips on a quiet fact-finding mission to India and on the latter's return to Washington the gist of his secret report to the President promptly appeared in Pearson's column. According to Drew, Phillips "recommended that if India was given the promise of independence it would throw thousands of soldiers into battle." This statement of the obvious naturally angered Churchill and also marked the end of the British hold on India.

When questioned under oath about this secret report, Pearson replied: "I got it from an Indian." Technically he was correct since the President is the Great White Father of the Indian tribes in the United States. It was common knowledge in inner intelligence circles that Roosevelt had personally "leaked" the report to Drew in order to hit back at Churchill.

The same was almost certainly true of Pearson's January 23, 1951, column on the Wake Island conference between Truman and MacArthur. In a pre-trial examination under oath some years later, Drew's partner, Jack Anderson, testified along these lines:

Q Mr. Pearson has stated you supplied him the material
   to be used in that column.
A That's correct. I remember that.
Q You did that?
A I remember that. It subsequently was picked up by the
   New York Times and they got a Pulitzer prize for it. So,
   I have cause for remembering this one.
Q That column refers to stenographic notes of conversations
   between President Truman, General MacArthur and Gen-
   eral Bradley. It says this:
   > "And, furthermore, stenographic notes made of
   > the more extended conversations between Truman,
   > MacArthur, General Bradley and the other mil-
   > itary men are still so secret that each copy is
   > numbered. However, I believe it is important that
   > the American people know what took place at
   > Wake Island. So, herewith I shall report some of
   > the conversations recorded in these notes."
A Well, the "I" in this case is Mr. Pearson, not me.
Q Pardon.
A The "I" in this case is Mr. Pearson, not me.
Q That is correct.
A He wrote the story.
Q That is correct.

And then the column proceeds to quote verbatim
from the stenographic notes which were still so
secret that each copy was numbered.

Q Did you receive a copy of those stenographic notes?
A I don't recall that I did. It seems to me that I did not.
Q Was a copy of the stenographic notes shown to you?
A I don't recall all the circumstances.

Again, the consensus in Washington intelligence
circles was that President Truman "leaked" the
Wake Island story, after "bugging" the interview
with MacArthur with a view to his later removal
from the Far Eastern command, secure in the
belief that no one would credit him with using a
man whom he had branded as "a sunovabitch" over
a nation-wide radio hook-up. As Drew put it later,
"Well, Mr. Truman and I have been on friendly

terms since then, and he has done me some favors." Marine biologists believe that North American eels migrate to the Sargasso Sea for breeding purposes, but this seems evidence that they sometimes get together in Washington.

So, also, when Pearson launched his campaign of character-assassination against Secretary of Defense Forrestal, he did so to strengthen Truman's tentative intention to install Louis Johnson in his place. Johnson had been euchered out of the Secretaryship of War under Roosevelt, partly because FDR could not muster the will-power to get rid of Harry Woodring. Bernard Baruch once described Johnson as "an able, ambitious, coarse-fibered man." Johnson had earned Baruch's displeasure for having, as Assistant Secretary of War under Woodring, drafted a plan for industrial mobilization. However, after the 1948 election, Johnson had valid political claim to a big post and he wanted the Defense Secretaryship. Drew Pearson, by hounding Forrestal, made it natural for President Truman to give it to him.

So it went with other stories. When Drew wrote about highly secret atomic developments, there was always the chance that his informant was David Lilienthal. When his column quoted from a drastic Eisenhower defense spending cut-back on March 9, 1953, it was a fair bet that one of the Secretaries of the Army, Navy and Air Force, or their Chiefs of Staff had slipped him a copy. For these and other indiscretions Pearson was investigated by the F.B.I. and military intelligence officers — but the probers always withdrew when they began to suspect whose finger-prints would be found on the document.

All of these didoes received an airing as a result

of the report of a 1957 Special Government Commission under the Chairmanship of Lloyd Wright, former President of the American Bar Association, on Government publicity and publications policy. The report cited several of Pearson's columns in evidence of news-leaks of classified material; Drew sued for libel on the ground that this implied he was disloyal or unpatriotic. In the course of his pre-trial interrogation on November 18, 1958, by Roger Robb, representing Mr. Wright, Drew Pearson revealed that he had passed the threshold of routine journalistic responsibility and arrogated to himself the right to decide whether a secret government document should be declassified. By law this power is vested in the President of the United States. But Drew asserted the right to overrule the President or his agents on his own authority. The following passages from the interrogation, which was filed with the Federal District Court for the District of Columbia on November 26, 1958, speak for themselves:

A Well, I think that Mr. Wright could have ascertained from, let's say, the newspaper publishers or editors in Los Angeles where he lives or in Washington from newspaper editors or others —

Q Ascertained what?

A The fact that I am not an unpatriotic person and that I do not, in effect, betray my own country.

Q Have you finished your answer?

A Yes.

Q Do your say that he could have ascertained that these columns he cited did not contain classified information?

A No. This complaint does not mean to allege that.

Q The fact is you freely concede they do contain classified information, don't you, Mr. Pearson?

A Much of it or part of its was certainly classified, but I want to come back to the word "classified" at that time.

Q At what time?

A At the time of publication.

Now, the word "classified" is a rather broad term and is used, as they say in the government, to cover a multitude of sins or a multitude of things they don't want the public to know about.

As you know, but the public properly doesn't know, the word "classified" may cover secret, top secret, any number of ramifications, and the stamp is sometimes affixed to a document merely for the purpose of covering up a political error or an error of efficiency.

But I have already answered your question. Much of this was classified in name.

* * * *

A Number 1: Because a classified document may not entail any security classification. A classified document is a rather all-embracing label which is placed on all sorts of documents.

Number 2: Every document, every publication, has to be examined as to the date, as to the effect upon the national security and the particular circumstances involved.

Q Examined by whom?

A It has to be examined by the newspaperman and in consultation with anyone at the Pentagon with whom he may in touch, particularly the offices of public information or press relations.

Q Is it your position, then, even though a document is classified secret or top secret, a newspaperman can decide for himself whether or not publication would endanger the national security?

A Under the rules of the censorship during the war, newspapermen did that in consultation with the Bureau of Censorship, who were also newspapermen. During the days of peace there is no law which governs this matter and I, personally, have made it a policy to try to apply the rules which we used during the war.

MR. ROBB: I would like, Mr. Pearson, a categorical answer to my question.

Would you mind reading the question back?

(The reporter read the question as follows: "Is it your position, then, even though a document is classified secret or top secret, a newspaperman can decide for himself whether or not publication would endanger the national security?")

THE WITNESS: My answer is similar to the one I just gave.
By Mr. Robb:

Q Is it yes or no?

A The newspaperman, within certain limits and with consultation and good conscience, has the right, under the
law, to decide what should be published.

Q Do you think the final judgment should be made by the
newspaperman?

A My answer speaks for itself. I think I have answered the
question.

* * *

Q And, as I understand it, your method of becoming sure
that such information will not upset the security of the
United States is as you have described it here, that is,
you consult with somebody; is that right?

A That is correct, in general. I can't say that I can give you
an answer regarding every case that comes up, but I think
that is the general rule.

Q You anticipate my next question.
Do you always consult with somebody when you get hold of
a document that is marked "secret" or "top secret"?

A The answer to that depends specifically on the document.
As I said a little earlier, there are all sorts of documents
marked "secret", "top secret", "classified" which may
have only to do with some inefficiency in government,
nothing whatsoever to do with security to the nation, and
I don't consult with someone if it perchance deals with a
trip of an Air Force general on a hunting trip in a private
plane. Sometimes I do. I would say 75 per cent of the times
I do even on a trip like that, but sometimes I don't.

Q So, at least in the preliminary stage you do make your
own determination as to whether or not the document involves the security of the United States; is that right?

A Yes.
When you have been operating in Washington a long time
and you have been operating through a war, when you
learn the rules of censorship and try to live up to them,
why, naturally, you have to make some judgments of your
own.

* * *

Q In your column for March 21, 1953, you quote at length
from an order from Under Secretary of Defense Roger

Kyes to the Secretaries of the Army, Navy and Air Force.
You start out by saying:

"This column has obtained a copy of the drastic
order . . . "

Where did you get that?

A   Jack Anderson, to the best of my recollection, brought in
a copy of it.

Q   Did he tell you where he got it?

A   No.

Q   Did you consult with anybody before you published that?

A   I don't believe so.

Q   Was it classified?

A   Most of those budgetary reports are temporarily classified.

Q   By the way, going back to your May 17th column, quoting
from the telecons, those were classified, weren't they?

A   I assume they were.

Q   Do I understand, Mr. Pearson, that you sometimes receive classified information which you consult about and
then don't publish?

A   Yes.

Q   In other words, you receive information which you, yourself, are convinced is properly classified secret; is that
right?

A   Yes.

Q   And you reach the conclusion that the publication of such
information would damage the security of the United States;
is that right?

A   Yes.

Q   Does that frequently happen, that you reach such a conclusion?

A   It would be hard for me to give you an estimate as to how
frequently it happens. It does happen from time to time.
It doesn't happen — I'll put it this way: It frequently happens in time of war. It does not so frequently happen in
time of peace, but it does happen.

Q   When you have such information in your possession, do
you take care that it doesn't leak out to some unauthorized
person besides yourself?

A   Well, there wouldn't be any way it could leak out unless
somebody rifled my files or —

With this assumption of executive power, it becomes important to examine the kind of secret

information which Pearson believes he is justified in publishing.

On January 31, 1951, he published a classified Chinese Communist combat bulletin giving an estimate of American fighting ability. Any youngster in Army Intelligence knows that our possession of this bulletin was a useful tactical secret and should not have been blabbed by a columnist. Yet again and again, Pearson asserted the principle that he would publish anything he felt the American people had the right to know. For example, on March 11th, 1951, he broadcast the following statement over the ABC Network from Munich, Germany:

Now the Korean War news: Stuart Symington, head of the National Security Council, has written a secret report urging that we get out of Korea altogether. He warns that our troops are too vulnerable, could easily be cut off by Russian air and submarine attack. The Symington survey has been sent to the Joint Chiefs of Staff for comment, but there has been no change in the decision to remain in Korea.

Nevertheless, he calmly denied that it could help the Chinese Communists to show that our war-purpose was weakening at the top.

On December 1, 1951, he also published a still exclusive report of defense mobilization plans to ban entirely the manufacture of automobiles, refrigerators, TV sets, etc. for civilian use. This false report was scarcely calculated to increase public support for the Korean Police Action.

When the Eisenhower Administration came in, Drew stripped himself of yet one more layer of self-restraint in his revealing journalistic dance of the seven veils. Take these random items cited in connection with his libel suit against Lloyd Wright:

Q   This column (January 30, 1958) starts off:
     "Pink-faced with fury, President Eisenhower verbally

ripped the brass buttons off his Pacific Commander, Admiral Felix Stump, the other day at a secret strategy session at the Quantico, Virginia Marine Base. Ike strode into the conference room while Stump was reporting on the Far East."

Q   Who told you what happened at a secret meeting at Quantico?

A   MR. DONOVAN(Pearson's high-powered lawyer): I direct the witness not to answer.

* * *

By Mr. Robb:

Q   — you say:

"Admiral Lewis Strauss, the Atomic Energy Commission Chairman is trying to hide one of the reddest faces in Washington. The Defense Department has just rejected one of his 'clean' H bombs because it is too dirty for tactical military use."

Q   I show you this column and ask you if it is your column and you did write that.

A   Yes; this is my column.

Q   Where did you get that information?

A   MR. DONOVAN: Object on the grounds it is not relevant and direct the witness not to answer.

* * *

By Mr. Robb:

Q   In your column of March 20, 1958 you say this:

"Secretary of Defense McElroy cut the Navy's request for Polaris submarines from nine to six at the personal suggestion of President Eisenhower. This was a very significant cut and in direct contrast to the administration's claim of an all-out defense effort, but at a White House meeting Ike questioned the military value of the submarines even though they'll be able to fire 16 Polaris missiles 1200 miles from under the ocean."

Q   Would you look at that and tell me if you wrote it?

A   The reason I am hesitating in giving you a reply is that technically I wrote it, but actually I didn't.

Q   Would you tell us what you mean by that? One of your staff wrote it?

A   I was out of town at the time and it was written by the staff and probably should have had their byline on it, but didn't.

* * *

Q   I notice in your column of April 24th, 1951, published in the Washington *Post*, — and I will show you a photostat of it — you say this?

"While the nation worries about Far Eastern war strategy, it can be revealed that spectacular new atomic weapons have been developed that can wipe out an entire regiment with one artillery shot or neutralize a city without killing a soul. For security reasons, only a general report can be given. However, it can be stated that new weapons are under way which may stop Russian aggression dead in its tracks."

Then you list three of these new weapons.

Did you write that column?

A   Yes; this is one of my columns.

Q   Where or from whom did you get the information about these new weapons?

A   I have no idea. I could give you a pure guess, which would be Senator Gore; but I'm guessing.

*   *   *

Q   I notice in your column for August 8th, 1950, published in the Washington *Post*, you say this:

"There's been no change in the President's ban against A-bombing in the Korean War, but in order not to get caught unprepared Air Force chiefs are working out all the details for future use — just in case. They want to be able to retaliate 24 hours after Moscow makes the first aggressive move. This means that lists of main bombing targets and atomic bases for launching B-36s must be all set."

Did you write that?

A   That's right.

Q   Where did you get that information?

A   I have no idea at this time.

Q   Would you say that was classified information?

A   No.

Q   You mean the plans of our military about attacking an enemy are not classified?

A   No, for this reason:

Number 1: It had been —

Let me see the date of that again, please.

August the 8th, 1950.

Well, there had been considerable discussion with our UN allies as to whether the atomic bomb should be used, and there was a definite decision not to use it.

Secondly, it is a well-known tenet of all military preparedness and practice to be ready in case the Commander-in-Chief, namely, the President, changes his mind.

Thirdly, it frequently happens that either the military or the civilian heads of the military will have published a statement regarding American preparedness so that the enemy will not be induced to push the United States too far, so that the fact that the Air Force was ready to use the atomic bomb, if there was a change of policy, was just a matter of routine, actually. They would have been remiss had they not been ready.

Q Whether they would have been remiss or not, Mr. Pearson, do you think that information as to the plans that they were making for such an attack might have been of some value to a potential enemy?

A Well, specifically, — I can't recall whether this pertained to that particular story or not, but I do recall that at one time — it might have been that story — came up, and I went into considerable detail with the Pentagon as to whether this stuff should be published or not, and I thought any details of it should not be published. In other words, I had the information as to how the bombs were going to be loaded, et cetera, et cetera, which I thought ought to be excluded. It may have been that column. I can't remember, but they wanted some indication of this published.

Q Where did you get the information about how the bombs were to be loaded, et cetera, et cetera?

A I assume from the Air Force.

Q Who in the Air Force?

A I don't remember.

Q I show you the column dated March 30, 1947, and ask you to read the paragraph headed "Burning Blackboards."

A Yes. That is one of my columns.

Q Yes, sir.

This column read as follows:

"While the Senate dawdled over the confirmation of David Lilienthal, the Atomic Energy Commission, of which he is Acting Chairman, hasn't been idle. Inside fact is that some highly important policy-making has occurred in recent days in this most secret of top secret Washington agencies. Carrying out the policy we proposed to the United Nations, the Atomic Commission has taken steps to reduce research on atomic weapons and increase research on constructive, peaceful uses for atomic energy.

"Significantly, the decision to cut down on military atomic research was fully approved by Army and Navy spokesmen at a recent session of the Atomic Commission. Extreme precautions were taken to prevent leaks. They even surpassed the secrecy of the Joint Chiefs of Staff during the war. For instance, a blackboard was used for certain formulas which scientists wanted to explain to the Army and Navy. When the meeting was over, these formulas were carefully erased. On top of this, the blackboard was burned."

Would you agree, Mr. Pearson, you had some pretty secret information in that column?

MR. DONOVAN: Just a moment.

We object on the ground that the date is too remote. It is 10 years ago, and has no relation at all to the columns in issue in this case.

MR. ROBB: Are you instructing him not to answer?

MR. DONOVAN: I am directing him not to answer.

By Mr. Robb:

Q I will ask you — I want to make my record — where you got the information you published in these paragraphs and from whom.

MR. DONOVAN: If you —

THE WITNESS: I have no recollection.

Less than ten years later, Pearson had removed yet other veils from his danse á ventre. In his pursuit of Bernard Goldfine, Sherman Adams's too-generous friend, he benefitted by the use of microphones to get evidence.

In his attack on Senator Dodd, he defended the right to steal and convert to his personal advantage by publication the private correspondence of a public man. This one is outlawed by the Constitution, except on the basis of a sworn warrant.

And on August 4, 1966, he published what purported to be a letter from Miss Frances Knight, controversial Chief of the State Department's Passport Division and one of Drew's many bétes noires, to F.B.I. Director J. Edgar Hoover. The alleged letter from Miss Knight warned Hoover against a press campaign against him on account of trying to keep an eye on American subversives abroad. Miss Knight promptly branded the letter as "absolutely false — a complete fabrication." Mr. Hoover said he had never received such a letter. Many Americans would prefer to accept the casual word of J. Edgar Hoover than believe Drew Pearson on a stack of Bibles; still others believe that anyone whom he attacks can't be all bad; so he was left in the position of having condoned; inspired or defended a malicious forgery.

Who Killed Forrestal?

When the late James V. Forrestal, our first Secretary of Defense and an outstanding American, went to his death from the tower of Bethesda Naval Hospital in 1949, it was said that Drew Pearson had killed him by his unrelenting press campaign of persecution and slander.

The last significant commentary on the "Who Killed Forrestal?" riddle is provided by the fact that, less than 20 years later, John F. Sonnett and others who had worked with Forrestal during W. W. II constitute the law firm which today acts as Senator Dodd's counsel in defending the Connecticut Senator against Drew Pearson. For them it was a duty to their departed friend, James V. Forrestal.

It is also noteworthy that the United States Government is currently erecting the largest office building in the world, the Forrestal Building, to house the Department of Defense. The Press Club's suggestions for a suitable building to commemorate

Drew Pearson are enlightening but unprintable.

Jim Forrestal's ghost still walks and haunts his maligner.

That Drew Pearson thinks nothing about the feelings even of the family of a recently killed Congressman was brought up on the floor of the House last year when he was caught jumping on the grave of a man who had dared to take legal action against him.

On July 10, 1965, Pearson had written a column which led off with the following venomous statements:

One important part of the Great Society program, cleaning up American waterways, got a boost when a Member of Congress was killed in a Fourth of July accident on a North Carolina throughway.

He was Representative T. Ashton Thompson, Democrat, of Louisiana, who had many fine qualities. In the opinion of the big chemical companies, however, one of his finest was his opposition to cleaning up water pollution.

Two days later, Representative Joe D. Waggonner, Jr., one of Congressman Thompson's Louisiana colleagues, stood up on the floor of the House and accused Pearson of maligning the dead. The following day, Representatives Cramer, a Republican, and Fallon, a Democrat, voiced similar indignation, pointing out that the late Congressman had had nothing to do with the delay on legislation to control water pollution. Waggonner also noted what Drew had failed to mention in his pre-funeral smear — that at the time of Thompson's death he was suing Drew for libel. Rep. Waggonner said:

In the Washington *Post* and in other newspapers published all over the United States last Saturday, July 10, columnist Drew Pearson dipped his pen in the blackest of inks to libel once again, the late T. Ashton Thompson.

Not content to having libeled Ashton while he was alive he now pursues his hateful vendetta into the grave. When he lived, Ashton took the only course open to an honest man when his character is besmirched, he brought suit against this hate-filled man, a libel suit that was pending at the time of his death.

Undoubtedly knowing that he is free of that suit and feeling safe in attacking the dead, Pearson has lashed out again in an article, the sum of which is, "Now that he is gone, maybe we can get something done.

Were he here before me, I would say, "Attack the living if you want with your false charges, your innuendo, and your libel, but leave the dead to Heaven.

Has Drew returned to the scene? Does he seek another kill? For Drew Pearson knows that Senator Thomas J. Dodd of Connecticut has had a heart condition. He also knows that Senator Dodd is not running for office again for another three years. In view of his part in the Forrestal tragedy, this seems a legitimate question: Is Pearson trying to hound anti-Communist Tom Dodd to death as he hounded anti-Communist Jim Forrestal to his tragic end over a decade and a half ago?

Those who have observed Drew Pearson closely for years have been struck by his utter imperviousness to the results of his writing and broadcasting. There is a better case to be made that this imperturbability is a built-in characteristic, rather that he convinces himself he is an Avenging Angel.

One day when Drew Pearson had made a particularly vicious attack on the late Jim Forrestal, one of his aides told Jim he could take Pearson off his back.

With more curiosity than enthusiasm, Forrestal asked, "How would you do that?"

"We could feed him regularly some interesting information he thought classified and he'd play ball," the assistant told the first Secretary of Defense.

Without hesitation, Forrestal snapped, "I wouldn't touch him with a ten-foot pole!"

At that time, the then Secretary of Air and now Senator from Missouri Stuart Symington was known to be preparing to freeze on a bomber which was later called the B-36 four-motored propeller-driven Consolidated "Super-Fortress." Jim wanted a jet bomber instead. On one occasion, in fact, Symington roared at a Forrestal aide, "You tell your boss to stay out of my business on this plane, and I'll stay out of his!"

At that time Jack Anderson, then just another Pearson legman, but later to emerge as co-signer of Drew's column and heir apparent, was being fed the Symington line by some Air Force public relations officers. Anderson obviously saw two, to him, valid reasons for feeding out the Symington side of the plane controversy. It permitted Jack to toady to his boss, Pearson, by keeping up Drew's campaign against Forrestal, and, at the same time, to put out what he thought was "inside dope" on the Pentagon and the Air Force-Navy row, whose flames he thus fanned higher.

Jim Forrestal, for his part, could be tough enough when he thought it worth while. It was Forrestal, for instance who, after Pearl Harbor in the early days of World War II, insisted the Navy be rebuilt around the aircraft carrier and not the battleship, a move on which the "battleship admirals" fought him every inch of the way. Later in the war, Jim once verbally lashed the tough Navy Commander-in-Chief, Admiral Ernest King, to the point where a lone and unwilling bystander became embarrassed.

But Forrestal did not believe in fighting what he deemed unimportant engagements. And he was singularly blind to the danger of Pearson's attacks which "got him" in the end. A stab at dealing with Pearson was made without Jim's being aware of it. Forrestal was induced to invite Walter Winchell, who was then feuding with Pearson, to a tete-a-tete lunch in Jim's impressive office in the Pentagon. Winchell, it was well known, had regarded his brief connection with the war-time Navy as a high point in his life. He might be expected to take Jim's side against Pearson. When Winchell arrived, he was immediately shown into Forrestal's office.

To his Staff's amazement, not unmixed with horror, Jim Forrestal called in an aide 45 minutes later and asked him to take Winchell "up to talk to Symington." Winchell was fed the Air Force line and later published a bit about Symington and his ideas.

At one stage, according to Jim Forrestal, he, and the former envoy to France and Russia, William C. Bullitt; the Secretary of the Navy, Frank Knox, and Admiral King went to President Roosevelt with proof that Pearson had bribed a Navy clerk to get classified information. They asked FDR to prosecute.

FDR laughed, according to Forrestal's account, and said, "Now I've got him! From now on he'll be my hatchet-man." The President put the papers in his safe. It is a fact that Pearson suddenly turned around in his attitude to FDR, and there are indications that he acted thereafter under White House orders. At any rate, never thereafter did FDR have occasion publicly to call Drew a "liar." This story is given credence by the fact

official legal action was considered against Drew
as a result of his methods of getting information,
but was never prosecuted.

Part of Forrestal's indifference may have been
caused by another situation: Harry Truman suspected Symington of playing ball with then Senate
Republican Majority Leader Robert Taft of Ohio
and Truman persisted in wanting Jim to fire
"Stew." At this stage, six months before the 1948
elections, therefore, the continued Symington-
inspired knifing through Jack Anderson and Drew
Pearson must have seemed slightly ridiculous to
Jim Forrestal, who was actually protecting Symington from dismissal because he thought Truman's fears exaggerated.

Mainly, however, Forrestal believed that it took
a tough hide to stay in politics. "Most business-
men last about a year in Washington," he once
remarked in this connection. And, in his brief
discussions on Drew and in his actions, Forrestal
indicated that he believed Drew Pearson unworthy
of consideration, not even worth being held in
contempt. Whether this held true until the end, is
not known.

The point is interesting because Pearson brutal-
ly attacked Forrestal, who was an ill man when
one of his aides took leave of him in the early
summer of 1949 with the words, "Jim, your health
should be your first consideration." It was publicly stated, and printed, that Pearson had driven
Forrestal to suicide. If he did, the first Secretary
of Defense, war-time Under Secretary of the Navy
and one of the first of FDR's White House assist-
ants "with a passion for anonymity," became perhaps the first important official in American
history murdered by a poison pen.

Beginning right after Harry Truman's dramatic whistle-stop campaign and unexpected election in November, 1948, Pearson carried on an unrelenting campaign to induce Truman to get rid of Forrestal. Reading Drew's attacks today, they appear highly absurd. At that time, however, they had a whiplash because Louis Johnson, who had acted as Truman's Finance Chairman after sixteen others had turned down the job, was gunning for Forrestal's job — and he eventually got it.

November 23, a few days after the election, Pearson accused Forrestal of having armed Nazi Germany:

"During the years between World War I and 1933, when Hitler came to power, the banking firm of Dillon, Reed dumped several hundred million (dollars) into the Ruhr — Today the former head of Dillon, Reed, James V. Forrestal, is Secretary of National Defense."

This, of course, is a typical Pearsonism. Anyone who reads his statement carefully would understand that Forrestal's firm was doing this during the Weimar Republic, actually in an attempt to prevent Hitler's accession to power. Moreover, in this attack Pearson coupled with Forrestal, Averell Harriman, at that time Marshall Plan Ambassador and now LBJ's Ambassador-at-large but during the Ruhr financing a partner of another firm involved, Brown Brothers, Harriman. Also assailed was John Foster Dulles, later Secretary of State but at the time of this attack a Delegate to the United Nations. Foster Dulles had been an attorney in matters involving Germany for the Harriman firm.

Two days later, November 25, 1948, Pearson wrote: "Betting odds have increased a bit that

James V. Forrestal will win his backstage lobby-
ing game to stay on as Secretary of National
Defense.

"In contrast to his earlier statements that he
did not plan to stay on in the Cabinet, the dapper
Wall Streeter is now frantically contacting friends
to help him keep his job.

"White House insiders say that if he succeeds,
it will be a definite reverse of Truman's earlier
attitude."

Pearson then went on to assert that, as he
signed an order to increase the Army, Navy and
Air Force Reserves, "Truman dryly remarked,
'If Forrestal recognizes my signature on this one,
it will be the first time this year'."

Provocative? Obviously. Responsible reporting?
No.

And on November 30, five days later, Pearson
was back at it again, this time contravening a
statement by Truman's press secretary, Charles
Ross, that the President had conferred forty-five
minutes at Key West with Secretary Forrestal.
Pearson contradicted Ross in these words:

"Forrestal flew to Key West at his own request
but expecting a private, intimate chat with the
President. Instead, he found the house full of
guests and little chance to be alone with Truman.
***At luncheon, Forrestal was seated at the
President's right according to protocol, but he was
left out of the conversation. ***When the drinks
were passed, Forrestal took orange juice. The
others didn't. ***The truth was, Truman and
Forrestal stood together on the lawn chatting
briefly while the other guests milled about."

Pearson, who wasn't in Key West, knew the
"inside," an inside harmful to Forrestal, while

the rest of the Press, which had top reporters on hand, reported a long Truman-Forrestal conversation.

December and January and half of February passed with Forrestal still Secretary of Defense and Pearson still cutting him up.

February 18, for instance, found Drew reporting that unnamed Senators were "fed up with the hush-hush policy of the brass hats" and particularly with Forrestal who was alledgedly trying to keep secret the intense damage done to ships at the Bikini atomic test which, incidentally, was covered fully by on-the-spot representatives of the U.S. news media. Drew accused Forrestal, who personally witnessed these Bikini tests, with not "having paid much attention to the problem" while building $400 million in new Navy ships.

Two weeks later, March 1, 1949, found Pearson back on the Ruhr pitch again asserting that "Dillon, Reed and Company in which Forrestal was a partner, had extremely close ties with Germany before the war and poured millions into German cartels which later munitioned Hitler's Army."

Drew was apparently frantic because Forrestal was still in office, so, he now conveniently forgot that anything Dillon, Reed did was before 1933 when Hitler took power. Then the Stinnes controlled Essen and the effort, it bears repeating, was to save the Weimar Republic. Pearson also forgot, equally conveniently, that Forrestal was one of the top command in the U.S. war effort against Hitler.

These are indicative of Pearson's persistent and unrelenting attacks on Forrestal to induce Truman to drop a man who all his close friends now knew to be very, very ill. On January 4, 1949, for example, Pearson had not only linked Forrestal to pouring "millions into Germany" but "in backing the military in the struggle against the civilians in the War Production Board" a casual comment on a still unknown struggle.

Drew also accused Forrestal of waging a "vigorous if poorly concealed campaign as Secretary of the Navy against then Senator Truman's proposed unification of the Army and Navy." It was sufficiently concealed, in fact, so that Truman appointed Forrestal first Secretary of Defense and, long kept Forrestal as one of his most trusted and able lieutenants.

On May 22, 1949, Forrestal — who had been replaced by Louis Johnson as Secretary of Defense shortly before and whose nervous deterioration building up for almost two years had come to a climax and led to his being flown to Bethesda from Florida — fell to his death, an apparent suicide, from the Bethesda Naval Hospital tower. According to the Congressional Record it was stated on the floor of Congress that Drew, because of this consistent and persistent attacks, had caused Forrestal's "suicide."

Pearson continued to attack Forrestal even after he had entered Bethesda Naval Hospital in the Washington suburbs.

Just seventeen days before Forrestal's strange death, Marquis Childs records in his column of May 5, 1949, that in a broadcast, "Pearson described Forrestal as 'out of his mind.'" To prove this point, Drew reported from Washington that at Hobe Sound, Florida, just after his retirement, Forrestal heard a fire siren and rushed into the streets shouting, "The Russians are attacking."

This report is still, nearly 20 years later, a Pearson exclusive.

Truman himself termed Forrestal a casualty of World War II. Certainly many years of over-work for the nation under the pressure of war had taken their toll as Jim directed, pushed and oversaw the creation of by far the largest Navy in the world's history, a Navy that stretched in a straight line over 350 miles of sea as it moved about in the final days of the Pacific war. This, and an insoluble family problem no doubt played their role in what happened to Forrestal. He had remarked on several occasions, "If you're not ready to leave Washington tomorrow, you are no use here," meaning that you could not make the hard decisions sometimes necessary. A physically well Forrestal certainly would not have waited to be replaced.

Whether Pearson's publicity campaign against Forrestal did play a major role in his death is problematical. Remorse has been no more evident than charity in Pearson. One of his singular qualities, as noted, is his imperviousness to the results of his "news" activities.

Pearson had based his years-long campaign of calumny against Forrestal on a completely false tale. In his column and on hundreds of broadcast stations, Pearson accused Forrestal of running away and leaving his wife to deal with holdup men one dark night in New York City.

"I would state," said Pearson, "that a man who runs out the back door of his house into the alley, leaving his wife to deal with a jewel robber alone, would not appear to have the courage or chivalry to be the best Secretary of National Defense."

The Forrestal jewel robbery had occurred July 2, 1937, some time before the Forrestals moved from New York to Washington. New York City detectives Tom Tunney and Ruddy McLaughlin broke the case when a thief, whom they had arrested for another crime, confessed to the Forrestal robbery.

Herman Stichman, later Chairman of the New York State Housing Authority, handled the prosecution of the thief in November, 1940.

Jim Forrestal, Stichman said, was asleep inside the house the Forrestals occupied on Beekman place when the holdup took place outside at about 2 A.M. and did not know what had happened until afterwards.

Mrs. Forrestal had passed the evening with friends at the Hotel Plaza's Persian Room. At about a quarter of two, she got into the car of Richard B. W. Hall who escorted her home. When Mr. Hall's chauffeur-driven car pulled up at the curb at Beekman Place, Mrs. Forrestal reported:

"Instead of the chauffeur opening the door, a man jumped in back with us. He said, 'This is no joke. It's a stick-up!' I told him this was a silly way to make a living.

"He had a gun. The gun was pushed up at Mr. Hall. There was another man with the chauffeur. At one point, there were two men in the back of the car; both had guns."

Mrs. Forrestal stated that she saw four men in all. They got her jewelry, assessed at $50,000. When they left, she rushed into the house, awoke and notified her husband and then called the police.

Not only was Pearson's story false, he proved it himself with his detail. The Forrestal house was on the east side of Beekman Place, and there is no

alley in or behind this block through which Forrestal could have fled, as Pearson stated he did
even if he had been in the car at the time of the
holdup.

On May 17, 1944, about five years before Forrestal's death, Pearson stated in another column:

"The General Electric Company has developed
a new listening device on the principle of a dictaphone by which outside parties can pick up conversations as far as three miles away. The device
is extremely sensitive and does not need to have a
dictaphone planted in the room where the conversation is taking place." Perhaps this was wishful
thinking for Drew has never scorned "bugs." In
fact, his aide Jack Anderson was once caught in
hilarious circumstance in flagrante delicto.

"General Motor's ex-president, Charlie Wilson,
efficient vice-chairman of the War Production
Board," Drew continued, "happened to have one of
these devices and one night he tuned it in on the
Forrestal home."

Wilson then, according to Pearson, eavesdropped
on a "Council of War" at which Forrestal, Bernard
Baruch and Robert Patterson, then Under Secretary
and later Secretary of War, and "one or two high
ranking Army officers criticized the Administration, including the President himself * * *."

"The criticism of the Commander-in-Chief was
so vigorous that Wilson and Donald Nelson (Chairman of the War Production Board) took a transcript to the White House.

"The President (Roosevelt) seemed to enjoy
the story. His chief comment was: 'Lock up the
transcript in a safe place and keep it there.
Someone will try to steal it'."

Pearson prefaced this column with the words

"Very few people know of an incident which occurred a little over a year ago at Forrestal's Georgetown mansion." This was the one true remark in the column; the incident Pearson reported in such detail just did not take place.

On May 27, under threat of action by Mr. Wilson, Pearson was forced to sign a memorandum that Wilson did not use any device to listen in on any such conversation and to publish a retraction. This Drew did on May 30. Mr. Wilson was, in fact, such a close friend of Jim Forrestal that he helped arrange the details of his funeral.

Although Forrestal's death was announced as a "suicide," a Catholic priest officiated at the burial service. This is against usual Church practice in the case of suicide and adds a queer footnote to the strange death of one of our most prominent contemporary Americans.

Drew Pearson can take it either way he chooses: if Forrestal was not a suicide, then Drew has wantonly libeled the memory of a dead man; if Forrestal did in fact kill himself while of unsound mind, then Drew helped drive him to insanity and suicide and hence bears a moral responsibility for the death of an outstanding American patriot and dedicated public servant.

Jim Forrestal's ghost, like Banquo's, still walks and may yet destroy Macbeth.

The Tool Of Special Interests

Forrestal's death marked the end of an era for the Washington Merry-Go-Round: It confirmed Drew Pearson's status as a political big game hunter; it also covered up the central secret of his power, the fact that he, who freely accused others of venality, nepotism and corruption, was himself the tool of special interests and was exacting a high market-price for his services to his successive employers. All this without faltering in his pose as a disinterested public servant, a posture enlivened by a policy of timely shifts in paymasters to suit changing opportunities.

If it is true that no man is a hero to his valet, it follows that no valet is a hero to his master. Consequently, the only way a valet can be a hero to himself is by timely, calculated betrayal of his successive employers. Only by treachery can a lackey pride himself on his independence.

Drew Pearson originally popularized the legend that he was a journalist of great courage and personal independence, who did not hesitate to attack anyone, however lofty his position or respected his reputation. His self serving unsigned appraisal of himself in the original *Washington Merry-Go-Round* made this unblushingly clear. He stated:

> Drew Pearson, the *Sun's* expert on foreign affairs, has the reputation of knowing more about the State Department than most of the people who run it, and to a considerable extent this is true. . . He is the State Department's severest critic, yet because its members either fear him or value his opinion, he is taken into their confidence on many important international moves. Because of his independence he is either loved or hated; there is no middle ground of affection where Pearson is concerned.

The truth is that Drew has been about as independent as the third assistant vice-president of the Chase-Manhattan Bank. He has always been a hired hatchet-man, for one President or another, for Big Business or for Big Labor, and has maintained the illusion of integrity by the speed with which he stabs those who have employed him, the moment they begin to lose power or influence, and by the skill with which he picks his next paymaster before the old one has stopped twitching.

At least three Presidents had reason to believe that they had taken Drew Pearson into camp. They began by making use of him; they ended by despising him; he ended by knifing them.

When Herbert Hoover appointed Drew's father as Governor of the Virgin Islands, he may have imagined that thereby he had also blunted Pearson's pen. With the publication of the "Merry-Go-Round" books, the President was swiftly disillusioned but did not vent his chagrin on the father. If Hoover had been Pearson, the poor old Governor would have been fired at once. Instead, Dr. Paul Pearson continued to rattle around in the Governor's Palace at Charlotte Amalie until 1934, when Roosevelt removed him. At the time, one of the odd para-doxes in the Pearson personality emerged when the columnist, a loudly professed foe of political nep-otism, put up a terrific fight in his column to keep his father on the Federal payroll and in time pre-vailed on FDR to give him a job in connection with the misnamed Federal low-cost housing pro-gram.

Pearson's support of the New Deal, including the preview of the Supreme Court packing fight of 1937 in the book *The Nine Old Men* which he helped Bob Allen to write, was exemplary. This, of course, was largely due to Allen but when Bob went off to war, Roosevelt swiftly got a new hammerlock on Pearson. This resulted from the already described attempt to bribe a Navy Department clerk to turn over to him the confidential personal files on the Navy's top Brass. If he had been prosecuted for this Drew could have been sent to the Atlanta or Lewisburg penitentiary for years, but FDR with-held his hand and tried to make Pearson conform to the necessities of the national war-effort.

This was somewhat akin to asking a chronic drunkard to follow the straight and narrow path. Drew interpreted his involuntary servitude to the White House very liberally. So liberally that in 1943 the war-time President had to call him a "chronic liar" for charging over a nation-wide radio hook-up that Secretary of State Cordell Hull and Assistant Secretary of State Adolph A. Berle, Jr., "would like to see Russia bled white."

Perhaps that was what Roosevelt had in mind when, on August 30, 1943, he wrote to Hoover's former Secretary of War, Brigadier-General Pat-rick J. Hurley, at Santa Fe, New Mexico. Perhaps

Mrs. Hurley had once snubbed Drew at a Washington dinner-party or her husband had declined to "leak" War Department secrets to the newspaperman. At any rate, Drew charged Hurley with anti-semitism and the latter asked FDR to call off his dog. Roosevelt's reply concluded:

. . . His (Pearson's) ill-considered falsehoods have come to the point where he is doing much harm to his own Government and to other nations. It is a pity that anyone anywhere believes anything he writes.

So much for Mr. Drew Pearson.

As early as January 1942, the conscience of the independent American press, William Allen White, dropped the Merry-Go-Round column from his famous *Emporia Gazette* in Kansas as likely to "give aid and comfort to our enemies."

Roosevelt's death in 1945 ended Drew's wartime servitude. Thereafter the sky became the limit. Some of his exploits included obtaining a verbatim record of a telephone talk between a Navy Admiral and the Attorney-General; intercepting the private letters of Miss Vivian Kellems, the Westport, Connecticut, cable-grip manufacturer and foe of withholding tax laws; helping force the United States to include the historic Crown of St. Stephen to Communist Hungary in the ransom paid for the release of businessman Robert A. Vogeler; publishing the London Foreign Office's instructions to Sir Alexander Cadogan, British Delegate to the U.N., concerning an alleged British-American-Vatican deal to support Spain's Generalissimo Franco; and quoting the text of a British Embassy aide memoir to the State Department concerning aid to Italy.

There was also an incident involving the leak of secret atomic information through the chauffeur of one of the Atomic Energy Commissioners. The man asserted that he was being paid over $100 a week by Drew Pearson but might conceivably have been lying, to conceal his real employer, since the case never came to court because officials feared the airing of additional atomic secrets.

These and similar free-wheeling reports did not endear Drew Pearson to President Truman. Drew had already written two columns making malicious fun of Bess Truman and had also published a false report that Truman had branded New York City Jews as "disloyal." During the 1948 campaign, because of his enmity to HST, Pearson supported Dewey and insisted right up until 3:00 A.M. on the morning after election that Dewey was winning. Then he turned around and, after a few side-swipes at General Harry Vaughan and other White House familiars of HST, worked hard with Truman to discredit and dismiss General MacArthur and to drive James Forrestal from the Cabinet.

Eisenhower would have nothing to do with Drew, so Pearson slashed at Ike's "soft underbelly" — to wit the self-righteous little New Hampshire Presidential Assistant, Sherman Adams, in the Goldfine case.

Pearson supported Kennedy but wasn't able to get a toe-hold in the White House under JFK, because of Kennedy's own personal crew of writers — Sorensen, Schlesinger and Salinger — the three S's.

With Kennedy's assassination, Lyndon Johnson became President; for a time there was every reason to believe that Lyndon had managed to rope, hog-tie and put the LBJ brand on the columnist. He gave a Federal job to Drew's own step-son and a White House social job to his daughter-in-law; he even gave a State Department protocol job to poor

George Abell, whose wife Luvie had been appropriated by Drew in the early 1930's. But, as will be established in another context, even this largesse didn't keep Pearson in the corral, and when the left-wingers abandoned President Johnson over Vietnam and flocked to the standard of Bobby Kennedy, Drew also declared war on the President.

This kind of "independence" of commitments morally binding on lesser men was made possible by the princely revenues Pearson began to enjoy during World War II while others were fighting and dying. Where the original Merry-Go-Round column had earned only $25 a week for its authors when it was launched on December 12, 1932, barely fifteen years later it had put Pearson in the millionaire class. In addition to the column, a comic strip "Hap Hazard" and a Latin American column, Drew had developed a highly profitable side-line as a weekly radio and later TV commentator.

His broadcasts were at one time sponsored by Lee Hats and he was even mentioned as among the "Ten Best-Dressed Men in America". For many years he was hired to conduct a radio and television program for the Retail Clerks Association and *Variety* estimated his weekly take at $5,000. As a result of these and other perquisites, the Standing Committee of Senate Press Gallery Correspondents called him up on charges and threatened to cancel his Congressional press privileges for violating the rule against a Congressional correspondent taking money on the side. Drew barely wriggled out of this one, by a one-vote margin of the Committee, on the plea that, after years in the Washington press corps, he was ignorant of this elementary safeguard against subsidized reporting on Capitol Hill. He did not, however, see fit to inform his editors or public that, while he was lashing out at Big Business he was in the pay of a labor union, or that, when he refrained from attacking the hat industry, he was being paid by a prominent hat manufacturer.

In other words, the man who preached austerity to Congressmen and Cabinet officers and warned Senators against "conflicts of interest," was himself the tool of special interests, not counting the various Presidents who bought and paid for his services in political coinage. Drew was swift to point out, for example, that Senator Dodd of Connecticut was supported by the Hartford insurance community, but he never informed that public that he himself was being subsidized by Big Labor or by Business. Perhaps this reticence was because he did not regard these payments as subsidies but as tribute. In any case, by 1948, he was in Big Business. As a colleague pointed out at the time: "He pretends to be a poor man, criticizing the rich. Actually, he's a rich man."

How rich is a secret between himself and the Internal Revenue Service. However, in 1948, he told an interviewer that his gross income was about $325,000 a year, of which $225,000 was for radio broadcasting and $100,000 from his column. His Georgetown office payroll for secretaries and leg-men ran to about $2,500 a month, and he reckoned his net income at $70,000 a year, leaving over $220,000 for "other expenses." Stated another way, he used over two-thirds of his reported gross-income for promotion, news-gathering, expense-accounts, entertainment, cultivation of news-sources, champagne parties, etc.

For one who frowns on junketing Congressmen

and once accused the late Jim Forrestal of escaping $95,000 income taxes "by a subterfuge company in Canada," these "other expenses" would make the Rev. Adam Clayton Powell turn green with envy. Maybe Drew has something on somebody high up in the Internal Revenue Service?

All of this leads up to a blunt question: Drew Pearson may not have been much of a hero to the Presidents he served or stabbed, but is he a hero to himself? Is he taking orders from that part of his character which normal people instinctively distrust, fear and despise? One of his few close newspaper acquaintances once described Drew as "half evangelist and half blackleg." Does the evangelist sometimes loathe himself for taking orders from the blackleg?

A few instances suggest that, instead of being a free agent, Drew Pearson is actually the slave of the most vicious tyrant any man can serve: himself. It is rumored that his vendetta against the late Senator Millard Tydings of Maryland, whom, believe it or not, he helped hound out of public life with the assistance of Senator Joe McCarthy, began in rivalry for the favors of an unmarried Georgetown girl who had turned Drew down. His extravagant enthusiasm for the former Chilean Ambassador began when Davila tipped him off to the Dolly Gann story early in the Hoover Administration. Thanks to Drew, the United States Government went into social convulsions over the question of whether Alice Longworth, as wife of the Speaker of the House, outranked Mrs. Gann, the Vice-President's sister and official hostess, in the seating arrangements at official dinners. Whereas nature seemed already to have decided where ladies should sit, this childish squabble

really launched Pearson's career as an exposer
of those drawing-room and boudoir secrets which
the laws of hospitality and ordinary good breeding
are supposed to keep private.

It is of interest to note that at a dinner-party
given by Illinois' famous Congressman-at-large,
Ruth Hanna McCormick, an extra waiter was observed taking notes and, when questioned, said
that he had been hired by Drew Pearson to report
what was said at the dinner-table. It is also alleged that his vendetta against Forrestal actually
originated in a remark the latter made at a White
House session, to the effect that if Drew was listening in he'd say one thing but that if the room
hadn't been bugged by Drew he'd say another. This
quip got back to Pearson and is believed by some
to be the origin of the columnist's antagonism for
a fine public servant. Maybe, however, it was
Forrestal's effort to have FDR put Pearson in jail.

Congressman Michael J. Kirwan of Youngstown,
Ohio, was once asked to help place the "Merry-
Go-Round" column in the Youngstown *Vindicator*.
The paper was Republican, Mike was a Democrat,
and he did not see his way to asking a favor from
a publisher who was opposed to him politically.
Thereafter, Drew Pearson attacked Kirwan with
tremendous energy, going so far as to campaign
for the Congressman's antagonist in the Ohio
primary, and implying that Kirwan had sold out
to U. S. Steel by agreeing to the deepening of the
Delaware River, as Chairman of the Public Works
Subcommittee of the House Appropriations Committee. The alleged pay-off was a small-salaried
job for Mike's son. This looked bad until you considered that if Kirwan had been that kind of crook
he would have been smart enough to take a much

larger consideration from the company whose ore-ships needed to navigate the river.

More suggestive evidence of Drew's subservience to his own whims, petty dislikes, fears, ambitions and power-grabs, is provided by his one real contribution to public policy — the Friendship Train which he suggested, organized, helped finance and accompanied to distribute carloads of American food to hungry Western Europe after World War II. This was the seed of CARE, the enlistment of private rather than government funds to finance people-to-people relief in the post-war period. It was a real achievement for which he was justifiably praised at the time. In fact, among other honors, he collected the French Legion of Honor, Norway's Medal of St. Olaf, and the Star of Italian Solidarity. He also got honorary degrees from two colleges.

This impressive personal contribution to post-war reconciliation is understandable if one recalls that, at that very time when he was being noble on the world-stage, he had just successfully kidnapped the "Merry-Go-Round" column from its originator and swindled partner, Bob Allen, and that he also just soft-talked his only daughter into selling him her 285-acre Maryland farm to him for a tenth of its value. The Freudians have much to say of "compensation." Was the Friendship Train Drew Pearson's "compensation" for these and other personal betrayals?

This is a riddle for the psychiatrists rather than for a biographer. There had long been suggestive indications in Drew's obsessive love-hate relationship with Cissy Patterson. There is something odd about a Quaker who has his chest tattooed with the Turkish star and crescent. His intimates have

noted his fantastic frugality, in saving used paper
napkins for future employment as toilet-paper, and
his self-revealing phobia about using only public
telephones for important calls for fear that his
own phone has been tapped. One of his newspaper
colleagues once noted that "the only time he writes
anything good about anybody is when he expects to
get something out of it." Another observed, "there
is something of the wild animal in Drew Pearson...
his eyes are never off-guard."

Perhaps the most revealing commentary on him
and his work is a remark he once made to an interviewer, "If something smells wrong, I go to
work."

His nostrils are so eager to scent other people's
corruption — particularly in high places — that he
once told a group of Capitol Hill "interns" that his
real job was "to keep Congress honest." It is not
on public record that he has ever gotten a good
whiff of the undiluted Drew.

Does he have a secret, justifiable scorn for a
community and a civilization which not only toler-
ates but richly rewards a man like himself? Could
there be a sort of death-wish which drives him to
see just how far he can go before decent people
show him the door or take effective legal action to
cage him?

There is no outward sign that Drew Pearson is
troubled by such inconvenient doubts. Now and then
he writes a sort of folksy column to his grand-
children in favor of peace and good-will. There
have also been rumors that, having made his pile,
he is weary of mud-slinging as a career and would
prefer a more constructive approach. However, in
every age, the worldly rewards of Faust's bargain
with Mephistopheles have always been glittering

and there is always the pious hope that you can have it both ways, as in Boito's version of the legend: get all of the luxuries of life and then make a final dive for the odor of sanctity.

The Social Lion

At one of the tables over Connecticut Avenue on the third floor of the Metropolitan Club, Drew Pearson, tall and sleek, garbed in a quiet, well-cut business suit, may be seen from time to time having lunch, sometimes in company with Arthur Krock, Marquis Childs or Walter Lippmann, among the handful of newsmen who belong to Washington's most exclusive down-town club.

The Metropolitan is an ancient, subdued, but highly respectable place. In fact, it has a doorman, whose uniform includes an old-fashioned bellboy's round, brimless cap, outside the entry to bar those who should not enter. The Club's first floor ceiling is amazingly high, even by other-day standards. On the second floor, there is a hidden bar, a large salon with low tables for groups, a large library for members to read or sleep in, and, in the back, a gilded receiving room reminiscent of Old World foreign offices.

The top-floor dining room, where Drew occasionally is a guest, is usually filled at noon with our top diplomats, including an ex-Secretary of State or two, a handful of Top Brass from other old-line agencies like the Treasury (the military are largely confined to the Army-Navy Club two blocks away) and selected bankers, business executives and cave-dwellers — old Washingtonians with pretensions of one sort or another. Negro waiters in heavily starched white coats add a touch of southern atmosphere. The food is excellent but simple. This is a place for good conversation and elegant, if brief, relaxation. The Club draws the line at only two types of members — Negroes, Drew Pearson and other similarly barred individuals.

Watching Drew — handsome and today white-haired and white-mustached — chatting as quietly as anyone else, it is difficult to realize that this is a man who seven days a week prints venomous tittle-tattle about anyone and anything. He looks more like one of the senior State Department officials than a political key-hole peeper, sensation monger and scandal detonator. Here, if nowhere else, he is on his good behavior.

There was talk, some of it extremely heated, about expelling Bobby Kennedy from "the Club" when, as Attorney General, he suggested that Negroes should be admitted to membership. Of course, this talk came to nothing, although Bobby would certainly have been blackballed if he had not already been a member as an inheritance from his father, the former Ambassador to the Court of St. James. There has never been a chance that Drew could be elected.

In other parts of the social forest, he is more fortunate. Today in the minds of most Washington hosts and hostesses, Drew Pearson and his actions and columns have in some metaphysical way been separated into two. This is particularly astonishing because Drew has been one of the few of the Fourth Estate, aside from Society columnists, who ever gets much news at Washington cocktail parties or at more intimate dinners.

Pearson remains a celebrity and if there is anything official Washington goes for with a fervor more worthy of a small town than a world capital, it is a Celebrity. It proved this when it accepted Frank Sinatra at JFK's inaugural despite his syndicate background. Moreover, many are afraid of Drew and his poison pen and think that they can conciliate the columnist and broadcaster by entertaining him. Finally, Drew is most of all an "old shoe" in the Washington diplomatic game. He was in it before most of those now feverishly active were even thinking of going to Washington and before many of them were even born. He has been in the Washington social maelstrom — or Femaelstrom — for a long, long time.

Today, hardly anyone can remember that originally, as a youngster, an unknown Drew Pearson married his way into Washington High Society. High in the sense of long-hung game, that is. When President and Mrs. Coolidge moved, by invitation, into Cissy Patterson's Dupont Circle Florentine Palace in early 1927, Calvin occupied the room vacated by her daughter and son-in-law, Felicia and Drew Pearson. Felicia and Drew, indeed, were fascinated by the fact the parsimonious Coolidge brought with him into their room thirty pairs of shoes, an assortment of flannel nightgowns and about a hundred pairs of woolen socks. One pair of these Felicia sequestered for Drew as a souvenir.

This Patterson "White House" at 15 DuPont Circle was built by Cissy's father and mother and furnished without regard to expense. Virtually everything in it came from Italy, France or Tiffany's. It is white marble, four stories tall and of Florentine style inside and out.

In those days at the left of the first floor entrance was a library and smoking room; at the right a reception room with kitchen behind. A huge marble staircase rose majestically from an immense central hall. A 25 by 10 foot Gobelin tapestry on one vaulted wall depicted, appropriately, a hunting scene, because on the opposite wall of the stairway hung the heads of elk, mountain deer, caribou and mountain lions killed in Jackson Hole by Drew's mother-in-law. This was long before she tried to add his head to her collection after a change of heart triggered by Drew's published remarks about the oft-changed pink chiffon sheets on which she slept.

The dining room on the second floor ran the entire length of the P Street side of the house, and sixty guests could easily be seated in it. It was then decorated in rose tapestry paper and had five windows. Also on this floor, appropriately furnished in the period of the Sun King of France, Louis XIV, was the adjoining hall with balcony attached. There was also a library to which the men could retire after a formal dinner. A small room which connected the dining hall and ball room was not so small that Drew's mother-in-law, Cissy, had been married in it to her first husband, Polish Count Gizycki.

The bedroom from which President Coolidge evicted Felicia and Drew had a fire-place and adjoining study and a bathroom with many mirrors,

as did the large attached room occupied by the
First Lady, Grace Coolidge. This, with other
bedrooms, was on the third floor — Charles A.
Lindbergh occupied one of these as President
Coolidge's guest on the flier's return from his
epochal flight across the Atlantic. Lindbergh's
presence drew crowds which the Coolidges never
came near to equalling.

Eventually, when spending more and more of
her time at rural Dower House in nearby Maryland,
Cissy Patterson was to refer to the Dupont Circle
house where her daughter and Drew lived with
her, as "The Movie Palace," a touch of contempt
in her voice. One gets some idea of its magnifi-
cence when she thus contrasted it with the Dower
House which she equipped with a greenhouse,
swimming pool, stables for horses, furnished with
a slate-blue drawing room, a dining room whose
walls were covered with thousands of dollars
worth of midnight blue silk wall-paper and which
she sprinkled throughout with antique furniture.

As one of Washington's free-wheeling hostesses,
Cissy commanded the eager presence of cabinet
officers, senators, congressmen, diplomats and
"cave-dwellers" like Alice Longworth who had
been married in the White House when Theodore
Roosevelt, her father, was President.

This was a profitable background for the son
of an obscure college professor with his way to
make. No wonder that when he frequented the
Latin American Embassies when few others were
so doing in search of news for the *Baltimore Sun,*
the Latin American diplomats were delighted to
welcome Drew. In some cases, that was the way
they themselves broke into Washington Society;
Drew got them invited to his mother-in-law's

house.

Despite the later propaganda about the parties of Perle Mesta, who became the subject of a Broadway musical when Truman's ambassador to Luxembourg, and of lavish Gwen Cafritz, Washington's foreign embassies have always been the center of the "best" Washington social life.

In those days, particularly, the British Embassy was the creme de la creme of diplomatic society and beyond that, usually depending upon the charm of the envoy or ambassadress or the bachelor Ambassador, other foreign missions became "chic" for a year or so, changing in popularity about as often as restaurants in Paris. At one stage, the French Embassy was very popular; two years later the Brazilian was tops and, once briefly, when it had a handsome and dashing young bachelor ambassador, the Finnish topped them all, particularly when the staid wives of stuffed shirt officials found the envoy would make a pass at them when their spouse's backs were turned, something very reassuring to an aging woman, however pure.

Almost anyone who was anyone went to the cocktail parties but only the very important — the Secretary of State or the chiefs of the military services, the chairman of the Senate Foreign Relations Committee, and others went to intimate Embassy dinners. And top newsmen were invited. After the death of polished Dick Oulihan, long rated the leader of Washington social reporters, The *New York Times* had to replace his successor, the able political reporter James Hagerty, father of the lad who was to become Dwight Eisenhower's press secretary, because the elder Hagerty did not enjoy wearing evening clothes. Arthur Krock, accepted in New York Society for some years, replaced him, at first regretfully. Currently, the Spanish Embassy, presided over by the Marquis Merry de Val, nephew of a Papal Secretary of State at the time of World War I and his charming wife, is perhaps the tops. And, of course, whoever happens to be Dean of the Diplomatic Corps has a special social "desirability."

Because of her influential newspaper family, her title and her wealth, and later as a superb hostess and publisher of one of Washington's three daily newspapers, Cissy Patterson moved in these circles. Soon, so did her son-in-law, Drew, and she did not break with him until long after his divorce from her daughter.

Drew looked Levantinely impressive in white tie and tails, worn for the most formal affairs in Washington until World War II. He looked as one would expect the Ambassador from Graustark to look, more like a ranking diplomat than most ambassadors present. His dinner jackets were always of the latest cut and facings, his shirts the smartest and his ties the right shape, color, size. He was, and still can be, a better listener than a conversationalist and, of all things, Drew's personality adds a certain decorum to any social setting. Not even his best acquaintances (there is a chilliness about him that does not make for intimacy) would accuse him of being witty. None would ever call him the life of any party but his own.

After he became a columnist, of course, Drew's desirability as a guest was tremendously enhanced. It would be interesting to speculate about how many diplomatic expense accounts for costly dinners and parties have been justified by mention of an ambassador in Pearson's column. One suspects that the archives of foreign offices from Oslo to Johannesburg and from Tokyo to Rome and Santiago are filled with such justifications for dinners with multitudinous wines, expensive courses, choice liqueurs and cigars.

Yet, in this social hurly-burly of a city whose ranking personalities are constantly shifting, Drew had an early disappointment or two. A British envoy slighted him. So Drew organized a State Department Correspondents Association, was naturally elected its first President and personally sent out the invitation for a dinner omitting one for the British Ambassador. Drew then sent a dispatch to the *Baltimore Sun* gloating at the British Ambassador "for being peeved because he didn't get an invitation."

This elaborate revenge was short-lived. It gave President Hoover the excuse upon which Pearson was fired from the *Sun*. The British Ambassador complained, the *Sun* investigated and William "Big Bill" Moore, the *Sun's* Managing Editor, called Drew to Baltimore, told him off and, some say, physically threw him out of the office in firing him.

This social vineyard Drew has worked for high profit since his early journalistic days. When Cissy broke with him, Drew was such a social fixture that, even then, it was forgotten how he married into the society of what was then a sleepy Southern town and has since become "the" world capital.

One of Drew's victims, the late James V. Forrestal, used to say that the greatest leakers of information were some of the tops of the armed forces and a group of the generals and admirals trying to make themselves important at cocktail parties. Although he dodged these parties like the plague, Forrestal was quite right.

At one cocktail party given by a Scandinavian envoy, this writer heard one of our top Air Force generals say, in front of a female reporter for the Washington *Post,* that he was going to ship as many fighter planes as necessary to the ambassador's country. This was a moment of crisis and the envoy's country, next door to the Soviet Union, was a key to the crisis. Soviet espionage had been trying for ten days to learn whether we were prepared to give aid to that country. The uncertainty was upsetting all their moves as, at this stage, the Russians were being careful not to make the first belligerent move because we had the hydrogen bomb in production and they didn't. Fortunately the *Post's* girl society reporter didn't realize what she had heard; Drew would have, but he wasn't there that day.

Drew did hear and print a good deal, however, and used anything that would make a good story to help sell his column or broadcasts. At one stage when I was covering the White House in the period just before, and during, the start of World War II, Drew made a regular series of predictions on his Sunday night broadcasts. They seemed amazingly accurate, until, suddenly, I realized that he was breaking the release dates on material put out in advance, sometimes as much as a week or ten days ahead. The rest of us scrupulously kept the release dates because it gave us more time to investigate and write our stories and kept the news flowing. Drew, however, was predicting developments on which he held announcements in his hand — and naturally beating the rest of us. He was a Nostradamus who didn't have to guess. Officials were afraid to complain. I did complain to FDR and Drew dropped the White House part of his sure-fire predictions.

In this period, we all got so we hated to have Drew at a press conference or a diplomatic party held by experienced and astute diplomats because he so frequently broke confidences in print or on the air. Knowing in confidence what is about to happen can be a great advantage to a news reporter because he then knows what to look for and what the news means when it does break. Drew frequently killed all this for us. Most envoys who arrived in Washington were told they could trust the press. But, Drew quickly disillusioned many of them and ruined our reputation along with his own.

Pearson was a real expert, though, on finding a diplomat with an axe to grind, Chile's argument with Bolivia over the Chaco district is a case in point, and he took Chile's ambassador's side as long as the envoy would feed him information on developments.

Drew was a great expert, too, on the "cover up." Arthur Krock, who always seemed amused by Drew's antics, chuckled to me once about the way that "old Cordell 'Judge' Hull" would finally get so angry over Sumner Welles' feeding Drew material to use against him that he would complain to the President. FDR would then admonish Sumner Welles and Drew would publish a column mildly critical of Welles. That day, you would see Pearson and Welles lunching together at the Metropolitan Club. And a day or two later, the assault on Secretary Hull, whose job Welles had actually been doing and deserved to get, would begin again.

A reporter can pick up snatches or pieces of ultra-secret information at cocktail parties. Responsible reporters, being social guests, will either check them out for publication with one or more of those involved or, as judgment dictates, forget them. Mostly the latter happens because the best reporters want to build up relationships with news sources of such trust that they are recipients of information when it is ready to break. Drew's idea seemed to be that a bird in the hand was worth two in the bush. The more responsible Washington reporters would not take any side in a controversy. Drew proved himself willing not only to take sides to get "inside dope" but to take either side to get what he wanted.

This hurt him, and still hurts him, with the rest of the Washington Press Corps. However, Drew is always shrewd enough to have at least one diplomatic pipeline and usually more, going on "Diplomatic Row" — and ambassadors and staffs change often enough so there is always new gold to be mined in the hills.

"And if there is anything Drew wants, it's gold!" George Dixon, the late Hearst humor columnist, who was never afraid to beard Drew, once snorted.

To some those garden parties with soft music in the background and the drinks rolling may have seemed awfully exciting or become awfully boring; the dinner parties sometimes interesting but, as likely as not, stilted; the cocktail parties a thrill, or eventually frustrating because no one really had enough time to get through saying something or listening to it; the idea often was to be seen, rather than to enjoy.

But to Drew Pearson, who married into it, the varied, and often slightly weird Washington social

life looked as gold did to California's Forty-
Niners — something to be mined and mined and
mined — at least after almost 40 years, his hair
now snow-white instead of black, Drew is still
panning it out.

One can admire his dedication and his endurance,
while shying at his obvious motives. It is a good
thing that the food served by Washington society
is usually above par and often delicious. Of course,
it gets a bit rough when the Russians start swal-
lowing huge glasses of vodka without taking a
breath and then turn the glasses upside down on
their heads to prove they are really empty — and
they expect you to go along. And sometimes you
have to pretend to like some awful dish or drink.
On the whole, though, Drew hasn't had to contend
with the wooden chickens and galvanized peas of
the Chautauqua circuit. And maybe that has made it
all seem worthwhile to him. In any case, he knows
that, unless the food is good and the wines served
at the right temperature, he can give his host
and hostess a free ride on his personally conducted
Merry-Go-Round. He smiles, jokes and talks as
though he were a gentleman, but behind his bon-
hommie and savior-faire everyone remembers
"There's a 'Chiel' among us taking notes!"

For this wary acceptance Drew has prepared an
appropriate revenge. He may feel justifiably con-
temptuous of a society which admits him to its
dinner-tables and allows him to visit — if not
join — its clubs; he may wish to make sure that
no one will imitate his ambivalent role as curse
and celebrity. Whatever his motives, he has made
it sure that the social lion will be followed by a
jackal. In his choice of heir-apparent to the empire
of the "Merry-Go-Round," he has expressed his

final scorn for a community which accepted him as a social equal. He has groomed a journalistic barbarian to follow in his train: Jack Anderson, and whether Anderson be regarded as employee, pupil, protege or crown prince, he has already slimed his spurs in the Battle of Washington.

The Corso Case

A very tough little retired Army Intelligence
officer has finally put Drew Pearson and Jack
Anderson on the spot for unauthorized possession
and use of a classified FBI Document. It is the kind
of document to whose use liberal columnists long
have objected, a personnel report. The one sure
thing is that it was not handed to the two columnists overtly or covertly by the Federal Bureau of
Investigation.

Whether they can get off this spot, as they have
so many others, is the current Washington conundrum. Because the matter is now one of court
record, it is surely going to be harder.

Anderson and Pearson got hold of what is
claimed to be a "raw" — which means unevaluated
FBI file on Colonel Phillip J. Corso, retired, and
used it in their own rough way to attack not only
Corso but Rep. Michael J. Feighan, Cleveland,
Ohio, Democrat, whom they have openly attacked
for, according to them, having become too con-

servative during his many terms in Congress.

Colonel Corso had worked his way up from a drafted Army private in the first days of World War II to become chief of Allied Intelligence in war-torn Rome, a trusted assignee to the President's National Security Council and an aide to the Commanding General G-2. At one time, this almost tiny, thin man directed fifty agents operating behind the lines of the Nazi Army in Italy after landing at Salerno and Anzio and, much later, he commanded the first U.S. missile batallion in West Germany, a delicate job because he was stationed near the Soviet Zone and his missiles had live warheads. Corso had a key G-2 role in Japan during the Korean war and served on the staff at the Panmunjom peace talks which ended that conflict. He is still on the U.S. House of Representatives payroll.

Such an intensely active man, operating in the international and Washington fields, is bound to have made some enemies, be they political, professional or personal. A "raw" FBI file, carrying interrogations of many persons, would almost be bound to include adverse remarks. Corso made clear in his pre-trial testimony, he believed this had happened to him.

Corso decided to fight what he held to be a "smear." One lawyer told him it was useless because, even if he won his libel suit, Pearson had hidden his assets and had many in his wife's name. Corso was not interested in money but in his "honor." He sued, and employed as his attorney, Robert E. Manuel, who investigated the case of the Texas wheeler-dealer, Billie Sol Estes. Friends of Jack Anderson have approached Corso, with or without authorization, to advance the possibility of a settlement out of court. Corso has curtly rejected such advances.

One interesting point is that in some cities the column attacking Corso, and through him Feighan, is signed only "By Drew Pearson," in others "By Drew Pearson and Jack Anderson," which makes clear that the Heir Apparent, as well as the original Attack Ace, are involved. If Anderson wrote the column, or even if he just collaborated upon it, it is clear that the heir has managed to absorb entirely the Pearson *modus operandi* in employment of semantics. Take these exchanges:

Q. (By Warren Woods, Attorney for Jack Anderson): Now, Mr. Anderson goes on to say, "The Colonel, as he likes to be known, works out of the office of Senator Strom Thurmond, the White Supremacy Champion" — "worked out of it before latching onto Feighan."
Is this correct?

A. This is typical Anderson-Pearson writing. "The Colonel as he likes to be called" — I am a colonel.

Q. Well, do you like to be called that?

A. And I carry an identification. He uses it in a derogatory sense here.

Mr. Manuel: Well, is it a crime to be a colonel or to be called a colonel?

Mr. Woods: It certainly isn't as far as I am concerned. I am only asking the man if he likes to be called colonel.

The Witness Corso: This is a military address as a commander and my official title and I am allowed to use it. I am allowed to use the title of Colonel.

Q. (Mr. Woods) * * *All I am asking you is whether you like to be called by your title.

Mr. Manuel: Answer it.

A. (Corso) Yes.

Q. (Mr. Woods) All right. We have wasted a lot of space.

A. But this is derogatory. "Worked out of."

Q. And the fact is you worked out of the office of Senator Strom Thurmond.
Is that not correct?

A. I worked in the office of Senator Strom Thurmond for a

year and nine months. (His principal tasks, he testified, were in connection with the Senate Preparedness Sub-Committee and military matters, he has a "Top Secret" Pentagon clearance.)

Q. Would you regard Senator Strom Thurmond as a white supremacy champion?

A. It says it.

Q. Would you consider him a white supremacy champion?

A. No, and "before again latching onto Feighan" — again he (Anderson) uses that term which is derogatory. I didn't latch onto Feighan. I just went to work for him.

Q. All right. Now the next paragraph says "Attorney General Katzenbach furnished the Judiciary Committee with the FBI report which accused Corso of nothing illegal." Is that correct or not?

Q. Katzenbach did furnish him (Emmanuel Celler, Chairman of the House Judiciary Committee) with the report.

Q. And this report, to your knowledge, accused you of nothing illegal?

A. They couldn't. I have never stolen or done anything dishonest.

Q. "But it was so disconcerting that Chairman Emmanuel Celler refused to approve the appointment (of Corso to Judiciary Committee staff)."
Is that correct?

A. If it was so disconcerting to Celler, I think you would have to ask him. I am not in his mind. He did refuse to approve the appointment.

Q. Now the next paragraph says, "In a rage Feighan phoned the Attorney General and tongue-lashed him for turning the FBI report over to Celler."

A. If I know Feighan, the type of man he is, he is a mild-mannered gentlemanly type. This is completely false.

Q. "This is from the Congressman (Feighan) who has conjured up communists where not even the late Joe McCarthy imagined them."

A. That doesn't accuse me. That accuses the Congressman.

* * * *

Mr. Manuel: Did you find the statement where Mr. Feighan said the CIA was loaded with communists?

Mr. Woods: I found the statement in which he said there were communists in high places in the CIA (Central Intelligence Agency) and the State Department and that it's time to get rid of them.

Mr. Manuel: No, "loaded" is what your client said.

Mr. Woods: That's right. I think it's a fair comment.
(There was a luncheon break shortly after this interchange. Then:)

Q. Now again, on the subject of right wing intrigue, is it still your position, sir, after the luncheon recess, that you will not testify about the subject matter of your testimony before the Senate Internal Security Sub-Committee in 1961 and '62?

A. I consider this statement — as I said before, this is a typical Anderson McCarthyite type of statement that he accuses everybody else of.

Q. In substance, your answer is no, that you will not testify —

Mr. Manuel: The answer is that he will not answer these questions unless he is compelled to do so by the Court for his own protection; because I checked over the lunch hour and that is still Executive Session (secret) testimony and it has never been released.

This is illustrative of the sort of writing Anderson, imitating his mentor, does as a *modus operandi*. The terms "the Colonel as he likes to be known," "worked out of Thurmond's office," "white supremacy," when Corso's work was military sub-committee work, "latched onto", et cetera, conveyed an impression which Jack Anderson's attorney went to great pains to try to prove might be technically accurate. The courts must decide whether the phrases convey a false impression of a man who has been commended by J. Edgar Hoover himself for writing the draft of the Declaration of Caracas, intended to deal with Communist subversion in this hemisphere and who retired honorably from the U.S. Army as late as March, 1963.

The fact this case is pending in the courts did not keep Pearson and Anderson from continuing to attack Congressman Feighan; in fact, Drew made clear in one column that he was going to run

Feighan out of office as he claimed he did Feighan's predecessor.

Corso has one advantage that perhaps no one else who has fought Pearson and Anderson has had. Phillip Corso certainly does not possess the international experience of, say, General Douglas MacArthur with whom Pearson once settled out of court and then, until his death, attacked periodically. Although Corso has operated, particularly during four years in connection with the National Security Council, in the area of "big time" Washington politics, he is far out of the league of FDR and HST whom Drew attacked. The advantage of Corso, who was a steel worker before he was drafted into the Army, is that he operated in the same League as 007, James Bond, that "roll in the gutter" level of war and international politics where one false move may mean death and where knowing how to fight in the dark against clever and determined enemies like the Gestapo (Corso testified he got 10,000 Jews out of Italy) is all in the day's work.

It is interesting, therefore, to see how he placed Jack and Drew, through seemingly innocuous and highly defensive, almost cringing, testimony right on the well-known spot.

This is that spot: The FBI must either certify to a Court that what Pearson and Anderson submitted is a copy of a classified FBI report on Corso — or else. And if the President or the FBI wants to prosecute for unauthorized possession — well, read the interchanges about the alleged FBI report:

Q. Corso: He (Feighan) said Celler had received an adverse report from the Attorney General.

Q. Did he actually show you a copy of that report?

A. Not at the time. He didn't have one.

Q. Did he later show you a copy?

A. Later, with I understand, the comment of the Attorney General.

Then the key question:

Q. And I show you Defendant's Deposition Exhibit No. 3 for identification and ask you to say if that isn't a copy of what Feighan showed you?

A. First I would like to say something about it. The Attorney General had a cover letter with this in which he said that this is a confidential memorandum and is only to be shown —only supplied to the committee chairman and only to be shown to members of the committee or who else the Attorney General designates.

Q. I didn't bring the suit, Colonel Corso, but you did.

A. But there is a letter covering that, that this was a confidential memorandum not to be distributed beyond the committee chairman and —

Q. My question is, is that the Attorney General's report that was shown to you by Congressman Feighan?

A. Shall I comment on a legal — on a report which is acquired illegally?

Mr. Manuel: Well, I don't know the truth of it or not. It's not in evidence and I object to your asking any questions based on the report.

I understand it's a violation of the law to have classified material.

Mr. Woods: Well, do you direct the witness not to answer? He has already testified that he saw a copy of the FBI report to the Attorney General upon which Mr. Feighan said Mr. Celler had relied in deciding not to employ him with the Immigration Sub-Committee.

And the — one of the basic items in the alleged libel is whether or not there was a derogatory or unfavorable FBI report.

Now, the witness has testified that he saw such a report and I am asking him whether this is what he saw.

The Witness (Corso): I saw —

Mr. Woods: I think it goes right to the heart of the libel.

The Witness (Corso): I saw a letter which accompanied this report, which was over the top of this. So before I can discuss this report, I think I should discuss the letter which is missing.

Mr. Woods: We will discuss the letter which is missing.

A. (Mr. Corso): The letter said the Attorney General has

furnished this information to committee chairmen on a confidential basis, to be given only to committee chairmen and to members of the committee whom he chose to designate.

And Feighan talked to him and asked him to let me see it. And, furthermore, the Attorney General said that the reason this information is confidential is because it's unevaluated information and not to be shown or distributed beyond the authorized sources which he underlined.

Mr. Katzenbach said this. ***This is incomplete.

Q. Well could you read this document here and then answer whether this contains the same subject matter of what you saw?

Mr. Manuel: One moment, please. I want to lay a foundation for an objection.

Do you have a copy of the so-called report from the FBI concerning you?

The witness (Corso): No.

Mr. Manuel: Do you know whether this is a true and correct copy of it positively.

Mr. Woods: He hasn't read it yet, how can he tell?***

The witness (Corso): I didn't read this report but I say I must see first the cover letter which is part of this document.

Mr. Manuel: In other words, this is not a complete report?

A. This is not — there were three pages to the one I saw and that one only has two pages.

Mr. Woods: The Court reporter's record will speak for itself. I am asking him to read it now.

The witness (Corso): You are not — if this is an FBI report, you are not authorized and I am not authorized to read it.

Mr. Woods: Do you refuse to read the document.

A. I am not — you don't have the right to force me to read an FBI document which is illegally in your possession.

*　　*　　*

Mr. Manuel: I believe the record shows he (Corso) said there was such a report. He has not identified this as the correct copy of the report.

Mr. Woods: Counsel, to save time, do you direct him not to answer my questions.

Mr. Manuel: I direct him not to answer ***for the reasons which the record discloses.

There was one sequel to this questioning which was to have important consequences. Because Jack Anderson's lawyer went so thoroughly into Colonel Corso's background and Corso answered his questions except for the few dealing with national security matters, Mr. Manuel was able to question Jack Anderson *ad extenso* about Anderson's background.

Heir-Apparent

Jack Anderson, Drew Pearson's associate and heir apparent, possesses Drew's expertise and nose for scandal but lacks Drew's finesse, social grace and flashes of humane awareness. This is the journalistic consensus on the short, stoutish, man with thinning hair in his early forties who nowadays often co-signs or signs alone, the column of his white-haired mentor.

Jack Anderson is quite ordinary in appearance, yet he demonstrated the flashing arrogance which is part of his character when he walked out on a House committee hearing, and got away with it, after being refused permission to read a prepared statement. Anderson flashes to the attack with the viciousness of a coiled cobra but, when under attack himself, he changes color as fast as a chameleon; he can't remember; he thinks maybe, or maybe not; he is misunderstood, put upon. It all adds up to even more imperviousness than is Drew's, to a tougher rhinocerous hide than even Pearson has.

Certain parts of Jack Anderson's life are an open book. He was born October 19, 1922 in Long Beach, California. He married Olivia Farley, August 10, 1949 at Idaho Falls, Idaho, has eight children and lives in suburban Washington at Bethesda, Maryland. Yet many years of Jack's life are veiled in mystery, particularly those during World War II when, apparently, he suddenly became a missionary, then a merchant mariner and then a Far East reporter, and everyone was confused about his whereabouts including his draft board.

Because Colonel Phillip J. Corso, who is suing Anderson and Pearson for libel, permitted himself to be interrogated *ad extenso* on his own background during pre-trial hearings, Jack Anderson had to submit to the same sort of interrogation.

Under questioning by Robert E. Manuel, Corso's attorney, Anderson said that his family had moved from Long Beach to Salt Lake City, Utah, when he was about two and that he had lived in Salt Lake until World War II, attending Granite High School and the University of Utah in 1940-41, finishing one year of college. He said that he took courses at "either George Washington or Georgetown" in Washington after World War II while working but never acquired a degree.

Jack stated that he worked two years on the city desk while a high school senior and a college freshman and then testified under oath as follows:

Q. What was your next job after that?
A. I accepted a call as a missionary for the Mormon church.
Q. Where did you serve?
A. The Southern States.
Q. I'm sorry?
A. The Southern States.
Q. What States?
A. Georgia, Florida, Alabama.

Q. Where were you ordained?

A. In Salt Lake City.

Q. What Church?

A. Mormon Church — the Church of Jesus Christ of the Latter Day Saints.

Q. Any particular church? I am not familiar with the Mormon Church —

A. That is a particular Church.

Q. Did you attend any school of theology?

A. I attended seminary during high school. It is not technically a school of theology.

Q. What seminary?

A. Granite High School.

                    *   *   *

Q. What kind of courses were these? What was the subject of your courses? You say they were Old Testament and New Testament. Can you specify anything beyond that?

A. They were as broad as the Bible.

Q. And you were ordained a Mormon Minister?

A. There is within the Church but as far as outside the Church, there is none.

                    * * * *

Q. You did not take the courses looking forward to becoming a missionary?

A. No.

Q. When did you decide to become a missionary?

A. I didn't decide. The Church asked me.

Q. What time did they ask you?

A. Early 1941.

                    * * * *

Q. How long did you serve in these States?

A. Two years.

Q. Were you assigned to a Church?

A. I was assigned to the Southern States mission.

Now Jack Anderson was 19 in 1941, the year of Pearl Harbor. In other words, he was of military age and the purpose of the questioning was to find out where he was during this period and what he was doing. He testified he served as a Mormon missionary until early 1944.

Mormon authorities say he could not have been

"ordained." They said he was an unsalaried, pay-your-own-expenses missionary from December 20, 1941 — 13 days after Pearl Harbor — to February 22, 1944, roaming about the South, including Mississippi and South Carolina, as well as the States he mentioned.

Then Jack Anderson testified, still under oath, in response to questions, that he volunteered in early 1944 for the Navy, whereupon he was sent to and attended the Merchant Marine Academy at San Mateo, California, which Anderson described as "the Merchant Marine Officer Training School" for about three months as a "midshipman."

The Merchant Marine Academy states in writing: *"We have checked our personnel records and find no one by the name of Jack Northman Anderson has attended this Academy at any time."* The Navy, for its part, disclosed this academy was not "under the Naval Reserve." And the Merchant Marine Academy says it refers to its student officers as "cadets", not "midshipmen."

Q. You went to sea in the Merchant Marine?
A. Yes.
Q. What ship?
A. Cape Elizabeth.
Q. How long did you serve on the Cape Elizabeth?
A. Seven or eight months.
Q. Did you visit a number of countries, or what ports?
A. The South Pacific for the most part and India.
Q. This would be in 1944.
A. Yes.

The Maritime Bureau records do not show Jack N. Anderson as a member of this or any other ship crew.

Anderson then testified that, in war-time, he had left the Merchant Marine early in 1945 to become a reporter for the *Deseret News* of Salt Lake City and that he went to China.

Q. Can you leave the Merchant Marine at any time?
A. Yes. A student officer if he prefers to go into something else may do so.
Q. What part of China did you go to?
A. Originally to Chungking and then into Central China.
Q. Did you cover some of the campaigns in China?
A. Guerilla campaigns.
Q. The guerilla campaigns?
A. Some of these, some of the air raids.
Q. Did you file stories with the Deseret News on these?
A. Actually, I filed stories with a number of papers. I was accredited with the Deseret News.
Q. There were other papers in addition to the Deseret News?
A. Yes.
Q. Which were they?
A. I am trying to remember. When I was a missionary, I dealt with several papers and I can't quite remember what — I dealt with a number of papers.
Q. Can you remember any papers you filed stories with?
A. There was a paper in South Carolina. They were small papers, I can't remember.
Q. Were they weeklies?
A. I believe they were dailies.
Q. Did you file stories with the Deseret News that were published?
A. I assume so. I didn't read them. I was in China.

So here we have Jack Anderson shifting in wartime from Mormon Missionary to Merchant Marine, which doesn't list him, to correspondent for a paper of which he does not remember the names although he apparently arranged personally for them to take his output. This is unique in the annals of journalism, and likely to remain so.

Now, shades of Walter Mitty, on page 94 of *Newsweek* Magazine of May 13, 1963, Jack Anderson himself spoke of this period as an alleged correspondent with "the guerillas" saying:

"I was always looking for something but I never found it. I don't think I ever filed a story from there. Nothing big ever happened."

There are two rather fabulous footnotes to Anderson's Mormon Missionary and alleged China experiences. On January 17, 1951, Senator Watkins of Utah, a ranking Mormon, flayed Anderson on the floor of the Senate and voiced deep concern about how Anderson had been permitted to see a private telecon report between General Douglas MacArthur, U.S. Commander in Korea and the Far East, and the Pentagon.

And on February 7, 1951, Anderson reported he had by accident obtained a letter purportedly written by an American Army officer to a Red "Chinese Spy Chief." That was the last anyone ever heard of this affair. But shortly thereafter one Gordon Anderson, brother of Jack Anderson, was discharged from the Post Office for being incompetent and, suspected of leaking the contents of letters to his brother, Jack.

The questioning about this hazy World War II period of Jack's career continued:

Q. Why did you terminate your relationship with the Deseret News?
A. I was inducted into the Army.

* * * *

Q. Do you remember the time you were inducted into the Army?
A. They had attempted to induct me before the war ended but I was with a band of Chinese guerrillas behind the enemy lines, so they were unable to reach me.
   When I came out, they inducted me.
Q. Do you remember the time?
A. It would be sometime after the war ***I do not remember.

* * * *

Q. What service of the Army were you inducted into, infantry or what?
A. Stars and Stripes eventually. I think there was a brief

period that I was in the Quartermaster Corps.

* * * *

Q. Did you receive any decorations while you were in the
    military?

A. Yes.

Q. What kind?

A. Service in action in the Pacific.

Q. Did you have some battle stars on them?

A. No.

Q. You got the ribbon that everybody got for the South Pacific
    — yellow-orange?

A. It was a Merchant Marine decoration. I don't recall.

Q. Did you receive any decorations as distinguished from
    your service ribbons which everybody else got? Silver
    Star, Purple Heart? That is what I am talking about.

A. No.

Anderson testified that he was mustered out of
this service in early 1947 somewhere on the West
Coast. By 1948, he was "covering" the Pentagon
for Drew Pearson and helping Pearson in his re-
lentless attack on war-time Assistant Secretary
and Secretary of the Navy James V. Forrestal, now
in 1948 the first U.S. Secretary of Defense.

There are reports that Jack Anderson and two
other men did cooperate with the O.S.S. shortly
before Jack says he was taken into the Army after
the war ended on August 16, 1945. Despite the
mystery, the record is quite clear on this at least
-- that, being of military age, Jack Anderson saw
no battle service and did not enter the armed services until after World War II ended.

One reason Jack Anderson's life during this
period from 1941 to 1945 is so difficult to trace is
that he could not himself remember, either in this
interrogation under oath or elsewhere, the names
of people he served under or exact dates and
places. For instance:

Q. Did you have a serial number in the Army?

A. I am certain I must have.

Q. You can't recall your own serial number?

A. I cannot recall my own serial number.

But Anderson could remember *Stars and Stripes* even if he couldn't recall the name of editor under whom he worked.

In answer to questions, he testified, "The *Stars and Stripes* just wore a Stars and Stripes patch — we wore a uniform and a Stars and Stripes patch."

What adds to the mystery is that *Stars and Stripes* was published in Europe; the China-Burma-India-Theatre of war had its own paper named *Round/Up*.

Moreover, the Salt Lake City Directory of 1941 lists Jack's father, Orlando N. Anderson, a clerk in the Salt Lake City Post Office, and his mother, a housewife. Jack is listed as a student in 1940 and a reporter for the *Tribune* in 1941. Then Jack was not listed again until the 1946 Directory when his name was again listed at the family address on Fardown Avenue in Salt Lake City. That was when Jack was supposedly on *Stars and Stripes* in China or thereabouts.

This attempt to probe his personal background shows how adroit and impervious Jack Anderson is in parrying attacks upon himself. He is one, moreover, who does not bother about contradictions.

Jack came back from lunch after testifying about his alleged war-time activities and declared that the "band of Chinese guerrillas" he said he had been with were "Nationalist guerrillas." He apparently did not recognize any contradiction in immediately thereafter launching an attack against those he claimed had prompted the questioning, i.e., "The radicals of the Right who live in a nightmare world, a subterranean world, of half-light in which truth becomes grotesque and weird and distorted." That is the Anderson technique at its best.

Consistency has never troubled Anderson. He and Drew have recently lambasted the FBI for listening in on phones in connection with suspected criminal syndicate operations at Las Vegas.

And although Jack has stated flatly that he has never engaged in bugging, he may tell that to the Marines, but the Washington news media will not swallow it. Members were present when he was caught in the act of bugging a press conference.

On frequent occasions, in recent years, Pearson and Anderson have decried the use of "bugging" or "tapping" devices, particularly when they have been employed by federal security investigators. Anderson himself got caught red-handed in the act of "bugging" the room of a public figure.

In early 1958, the Committee on Legislative Oversight, a subcommittee of the House Government Operations Committee, chaired by Rep. Oren Harris (D-Ark.), commenced a series of hearings on Washington's regulatory agencies. From the outset of the hearings two things became very apparent: (1) With the 1958 elections hard-by, the Democratic-controlled Committee was out on a "fishing expedition" seeking signs of corruption in the Eisenhower Administration to be used as campaign ammunition, and (2) Drew Pearson and Jack Anderson had inside sources in the Committee or its staff.

The first series of hearings involved the Federal Communications Commission and were stormy ones, involving the highly publicized firing of the Committee's counsel and the constant "leakage" of information from the Committee's files to Pearson and Anderson, who continuously published "raw" investigatory material before any witnesses had been called publicly to elicit the facts.

This phase of the hearings dragged on for some months and the publicity value began to wear thin. Then, in a second phase, the Committee began to investigate the Federal Trade Commission and the Securities and Exchange Commission. They hit pay dirt almost immediately when it developed that chief White House aide Sherman Adams had, on several occasions, interceded for a friend with both agencies.

The friend was Boston Industrialist Bernard Goldfine. If he had been recruited from a Hollywood casting office he could not have been more perfect for the part of playing the fat cat businessman-on-the-make buying influence in Washington, which the Committee, with its eyes on the upcoming 1958 elections, had cast for him.

Goldfine was a short, red-faced, rotund man with the manners and style of living of a Middle-East potentate. He traveled about trailed by an extensive entourage. When ensconced in a hotel he would rent not one but a series of suites and fill them with his retainers, a fact that would have much bearing on what was to come.

The Democrats on the Committee took one look at Goldfine and jumped with glee. They had on their hands a sure-fire publicity gimmick and they knew it. Goldfine, as befitted one of his style, was given to showering gifts upon all who came within his sight and from whom he could expect some courtesy or service. He was almost indiscriminate in this respect. Bellhops, chamber maids, cab drivers, Senators, Congressmen and Sherman Adams all shared in the Goldfine largesse.

When Goldfine was called to Washington to testify he retained a prominent Washington Attorney,
Roger Robb, to advise him during the hearings and
to augment his already large staff of attorneys.
Robb, who had been Chief Counsel of the Gray
Commission, which investigated the security background of J. Robert Oppenheimer, knows Washington well.

Some months after the Goldfine matter had faded
away Robb had occasion to question Jack Anderson
and Drew Pearson in connection with a law suit in
which he was interested.

Robb: Have you ever used microphones and recording de-
vices to get information?
Anderson: Never.
Robb: Never?
Anderson: Never.
Robb: What were you doing at the Carlton Hotel last July
with a microphone and recording device?

Within this little interchange is a story that il-
lustrates not only Anderson's attitude towards the
truth but his methods of operation and indifference
when caught way off base.

Shortly after Goldfine arrived in Washington,
Robb was told by an informant that Jack Anderson
and Baron Shacklette, an investigator for the Harris Committee, had borrowed a tape recorder and
microphone from an electronic supply house and
that the two men were planning to use the device
to "bug" Goldfine's room at the swank Sheraton-
Carlton Hotel.

For several weeks, with this information always
in mind, Robb kept a careful watch on the small
camp of suites registered in Goldfine's name. On
the night of July 6th, 1958 his vigilance paid off.

It was a Sunday night. Goldfine, who had been

weekending at his Boston home, had flown back late in the evening and was lounging in his sixth floor suite. On the eight floor Robb sat in another Goldfine suite and discussed the hearings which were to resume the following day with public relations men who had been retained that day and who were occupying the suite. The PR men were Jack Lotto, a flamboyant former newsman with INS serving on his first public relations assignment, and Phil Brennan, a Washington public relations specialist with wide contacts among the Washington Press Corps. Also present in the suite were Andrew Williamson, a top Goldfine aide, and Bea Duprey, a Boston model hired by Williamson to act as a receptionist in the Goldfine press room.

Robb and Lotto were discussing a press conference which Lotto had called for just after midnight in the hopes of capturing the following morning's headlines.

Brennan, who had flown to Boston early that morning to escort Goldfine back, was eating his first meal of the day. Robb stood up and began to pace the room. As he neared a door set in the hallway, which connected Brennan's room with the suite's parlor, he noticed shadows coming from under the door. Getting down on his hands and knees, he saw a pair of shoes pressed close against the other side of the door which led to an adjoining room not part of the suite. He stood up and walked back into the parlor where he motioned to Lotto and Brennan to follow him into Brennan's bedroom.

Closing the door behind him Robb told the two men what he had seen. Brennan then opened the door and went out into the hallway. Getting down on his hands and knees, he stooped and peered under the door and saw a pair of hands moving along the rug.

He went back into the bedroom and asked Robb what he thought this might mean. Robb told him that he believed that an attempt was being made to eavesdrop on their conversation. Brennan then asked if there was any device that could detect the presence of a "bug" on the premises. Robb said that there was, and that a private detective, Lloyd Furr had such a device.

At this point Lotto left the suite to go down to the sixth floor and be introduced to Goldfine whom he had not yet met. Robb went down to the lobby and called Lloyd Furr from a pay phone while Brennan resumed eating his long-delayed meal.

Shortly thereafter, Furr arrived and began to unpack his equipment. For the next half-hour or so, he concentrated on the area near the suspect door and finally passed a note to Brennan informing him that he was getting a "feedback" which indicated the presence of electronic equipment on the premises. At about this point the press began to arrive for Lotto's midnight press conference. Brennan and Robb had returned to the suite and ushered the newsmen into Lotto's bedroom, which was the most remote point from the "bugged" door. Lotto returned and was told of Furr's conclusion that they were indeed being "bugged." Lotto then informed the waiting newsmen who had come to hear details of Goldfine's largesse to prominent public figures, to be on hand when an eavesdropper was caught in the act that they were being "bugged."

The press was skeptical and deluged Lotto with questions. While Lotto struggled to answer these, Brennan asked a photographer to come out into

the "bugged" area and get a photo of the door. The
photographer asked Brennan to pose looking under
the crack beneath the floor. Brennan obliged and
as he did so he saw, for the first time, a small
black object lying directly beneath the door. He
motioned to Furr and told him that he thought
there was a microphone under the door. Furr went
into Brennan's bedroom, took a metal hanger from
the closet, unwound it and fashioned it into a long-
handled hook. Going back into the hallway he slipped
the hanger under the door and, to the accompani-
ment of exploding flashbulbs of the photographers,
yanked the microphone and several inches of wire
underneath the door, and into the room.

Pandemonium broke loose. Brennan went into
his own bedroom and placed a call to the room
next door where the microphone had been placed.
No answer. Lotto phoned the Hotel's night manager,
and demanded that he come upstairs at once.

Brennan went into the hallway, climbed on a
chair and looked over the transom. He saw a small
foyer with the door to what was obviously the
bathroom ajar and the door to the bedroom tightly
closed. He climbed down, went back into his own
room, then went back out into the hallway and
looked over the transom again. This time he
noticed that the door to the bathroom was now
closed and the other door slightly ajar. He motioned to the newsmen who were milling all over
the suite to quiet down while he continued to peer
into the room. A few minutes later the bathroom
door opened; Jack Anderson emerged and walked
into the bedroom, a shaving kit cradled under his
arm.

Brennan shouted, "It's Jack Anderson, the Jack
Anderson that works for Drew Pearson." The re-

porters now gathered at the door and began to demand admission. A few minutes later Anderson and Harris Committee investigator Baron Shacklette opened the door and invited the press into their room. They told the press that they had merely taken the room to "listen to hi-fi."

When being questioned about the incident some months later by Robb, Anderson's testimony gave a distinctive illustration of how he talks under oath; it seems to make an eel look like an iron bar. Here is the way it went:

Q. What were you doing up at the Carlton Hotel last July with a microphone and recording device?

A. I was a newspaperman —

MR. DONOVAN: Just a moment.

We object because it is not relevant.

THE WITNESS: Well, I —

MR. DONOVAN: Unless you want to tell him.

MR. ROBB: I am sorry.

MR. DONOVAN: I say we object on the grounds it is not relevant.

THE WITNESS: I don't mind talking about it.

MR. ROBB: Go ahead.

THE WITNESS: The night of the great imprudence — you were there — an authorized congressional investigator, whose credentials are as good as J. Edgar Hoover's, was conducting an investigation. He was using a microphone as one of his investigative techniques, which, as I recall, you did in the Burlington Hotel once, — I don't know whether you had credentials or not — but I was there simply as a newspaperman. I did not operate or I did not use the recording device.

MR. ROBB: Just so that we have —

THE WITNESS: And I never have.

I hasten to add I have never used a recording device to get information — at no time.

Mr. Pearson's instructions are specific on that.

By Mr. Robb:

Just so we can have a point of departure, on the night of July 6th you and Mr. Baron Shacklette, the Chief Investigator for the House Committee on Legislative

Oversight, were in a room at the Carlton Hotel here in Washington adjoining a room occupied by one of the staff of Mr. Bernard Goldfine and you had, you and Mr. Shacklette, in the room a tape recorder and a microphone that were recording conversations going on in the room next door to you; is that right?

A. Mr. Shacklette had a recording machine. I did not, but I was present in the room.

Q. Yes.
   Who had rented the room that you were in?

A. Mr. Shacklette had arranged for it.

Q. Who paid for it?

A. To the best of my recollection, he paid for it, too, but I don't recall clearly.

Q. You mean your memory is vague on that?

A. Well, we had two or three rooms that we used from time to time there, and I paid for some and he paid for some. As I recall, we split the bill about evenly. On that specific room, I don't remember who it was that paid the bill.

Q. You said you had two or three rooms from time to time. Had you been in the hotel for some days?

A. No; no. We had come in — oh, I imagine I spent a total of three or four hours in the hotel during the entire time Mr. Goldfine was present.

Q. Didn't you have rooms there about a week before?

A. Yes.

Q. And you had a room adjoining Mr. Goldfine's room?

A. Yes.

Q. And you and Mr. Shacklette were there?

A. I was there; yes. We were there for a short time.

Q. Did he have his recording device then?

A. Yes; I think he had a recording device, but I don't think he used it.

Q. Who got the room you were in that night?

A. Again I'm not too clear on it. It seems to me I did.

Q. Who paid for it?

A. We split the expenses, the best I recall.

Q. And didn't you and Mr. Shacklette also have a room across the hall from a room occupied by Mr. Goldfine's secretary, Miss Paperman?

A. I have never been in the room opposite —

Q. I didn't ask you that. I asked you if you didn't get such a room.

A. I don't know. You'll have to subpoena Mr. Shacklette and find out about what he —

Q. Who paid for that room?

A. I didn't pay for it. I don't know who did.

Q. Let me ask you this, Mr. Anderson: Whose idea was that that you go to the Carlton Hotel and spy on Mr. Goldfine? Was it yours or Mr. Shacklette's?

MR. DONOVAN: Just a minute.

I don't think that is relevant. I object on the grounds it is irrelevant.

THE WITNESS: Whose idea was it that you go spy on these people in the Burlington?

I don't know.

MR. ROBB: Well, we haven't got that very accurately, but since you have —

THE WITNESS: I think I have.

The only difference is you ran the wiretapping or directed the wiretapping, whereas I was present in my case just as a newspaperman.

MR. ROBB: Since you have undertaken to put that in the record, you know very well the microphones installed at the Burlington Hotel were installed in our own room, not somebody else's room.

THE WITNESS: Then you ought to know the microphone used in the Carlton Hotel was used in Mr. Shacklette's room and not in anybody else's room.

MR. ROBB: Yes, and was the conversation —

THE WITNESS: And, as a matter of fact, it was stolen by you or your people.

By Mr. Robb:

Q. Was the conversation in Mr. Shacklette's room?

A. The conversation was there, as I recall.

Q. In Mr. Shacklette's room?

A. There were conversations in all rooms, I suppose.

Q. Was the conversation you were recording in Mr. Shacklette's room?

A. Where was the conversation you were recording at the Burlington Hotel?

Q. In our own room.

A. And you weren't in the next room eavesdropping?

Q. Sure I was.

A. Sure you were.

As I say, the only difference was you were doing the

wiretapping, whereas I wasn't. I was just a newspaper-man.

Q. What did you go to the Burlington Hotel for on the week prior to July 6th?

MR. DONOVAN: Burlington Hotel?

MR. ROBB: To the Carlton Hotel.

You said you were there.

THE WITNESS: Yes.

By Mr. Robb:

Q. What for?

A. Well, Mr. Shacklette was conducting an investigation to find out who you people had hired to dig up dirt on the congressmen on that committee.

Q. Did he call you and invite you to come over?

A. Well, we had been working on a story together, Mr. Robb. It is a common practice for newspapermen to share their tips with investigators and, in return, for the in-vestigators to work with them, and that is what was going on in this case.

Q. Who went to the Carlton Hotel first — you or Shacklette?

A. I believe I did. I believe I did, my wife and I. My wife and I registered before Mr. Shacklette arrived, to the best of my recollection.

Q. How did you register?

MR. DONOVAN: Just a minute.

I think we are going too far afield here. I don't think this is relevant.

THE WITNESS: I don't know what that has got to do with this.

MR. ROBB: I am trying to find out the techniques —

MR. DONOVAN: I think it is irrelevant.

THE WITNESS: I don't mind answering.

MR. DONOVAN: You can answer, if you want.

THE WITNESS: It is up to you.

There is nothing wrong about it.

J. Edgar Hoover has used microphones in his work. I presume that a congressional investigator who has credentials to represent a committee is entitled to use the same devices. I don't know. That's his business, not mine. My business is gathering news.

By Mr. Robb:

Q. Let me ask you this: You say that you and Shacklette shared expenses on this thing?

A. Well, I was working on a news story and I felt that I

ought to help pay for the rooms involved, and I did.

Q. Did you help pay or did you pay the whole bill?

A. Help pay. I think he paid for most of it, as a matter of fact.

Q. Did you put that on your expense account?

A. Drew, did I ever get that money back or not?

MR. DONOVAN: I think at this point I will object — it is not relevant — and direct the witness not to answer.

THE WITNESS: All right.

By Mr. Robb:

Q. Did Mr. Pearson know you were down at the Carlton Hotel?

MR. DONOVAN: I object on the grounds it is irrelevant.

THE WITNESS: I don't mind —

By Mr. Robb:

Q. He didn't?

A. He knew I was investigating. He knew the general story I was investigating. He didn't know specifically what I was doing.

Q. How long did you and Mr. Shacklette work together on this case?

A. Three or four weeks, I guess.

Q. Beginning when?

A. About three weeks before the incident at the hotel.

Q. Had you worked with Mr. Shacklette before on other matters?

A. Yes; I had.

Q. Did you work with him when he was Chief Investigator for the General Services Administration?

A. I don't recall any specific investigations that I worked with him on there.

Q. Did he furnish you any information from time to time when he was employed by the GSA?

A. I recall that I furnished him with some.

Q. Did he furnish you any?

A. Well, I think that the same arrangements that reporters have with investigators, many investigators — that if they supply the basic information that leads to an investigation the agency feels obligated to inform the reporter of the results of the investigation.

Q. So, the answer would be yes?

A. Yes, but whether he would have done it — it would have been the agency. Whether he did it himself or the In-

formation Officer, I wouldn't know. I wouldn't recall,
but the agency would have — any tips that I would have
given them — I would have gotten a reply back on it
from the agency, more likely from the Public Information
Officer.

Q. By the way, what happened to the tape that you made at
the Carlton Hotel or Mr. Shacklette made at the Carlton
Hotel on July 6?

A. I don't think it was working; no. At no time did I see him
record while I was there and, in any case, I can't answer
that. It is his machine.

Q. You don't know; is that it?

A. I don't know — in the first place, all I can say is I didn't
see any recording going on, and what happened to the
machine and the tapes and the microphone — I know what
happened to the microphone. I mean I know what happened
to it that night. I would like to know where it is now.
Could you tell me that?

Q. So you know where Mr. Shacklette got the recording
device that he used?

A. No.

Q. Did he tell you?

Several facts stand out clearly in Anderson's
testimony. He stated that he was only accompany-
ing Shacklette who was "conducting an investigation." But several years later Oren Harris would
tell Phil Brennan that he had specifically forbidden
Shacklette to do any bugging or eavesdropping when
the investigator had suggested that this be done.
He told Brennan that Shacklette was not on Committee business that night and that he believed that
Shacklette had been working for Pearson and Anderson on that occasion. Shacklette was fired by
the Harris Committee the following day as a result
of his part in the episode, thus making it ever
more evident that he was not acting on behalf of
the Committee.

By the time of the interrogation, Anderson had
changed his absurd story that he and Shacklette

had been "listening to hi-fi" and now claimed with
equal absurdity, that he and Shacklette were "bugging" their own conversation, as can be seen when
Anderson told Robb that "the conversation was
there, as I recall." He then changed his story again
and admitted that he was "eavesdropping" but that
it didn't really count because he was there only as
a "newsman."

Finally, Anderson had the gall to state the tape
recorder was not working at the time he and
Shacklette were caught despite the fact that they
had been caught only because Lloyd Furr's device
had detected their equipment in operation. It is
obvious that Furr's detection device would not have
gotten a "feedback" if the eavesdropping machin-
ery had not been in operation at the time.

Anderson also denied that he knew anything
about what happened to the tapes from the recorder.
But several days after the incident in question
Drew Pearson published excerpts from the tapes
in his column.

Other testimony from this incident reveals Jack
Anderson's opinion of "secret" information:

> If you want my opinions on that, —
> Q. Yes.
> A. — I will be glad to give them.
> Q. That is right.
> A. I think that all documents before they are classified should
> be studied by a committee of newspapermen — newspaper-
> men are as patriotic as Army officers — and I think these
> newspapermen ought to help determine whether a clas-
> sification stamp should be put on.
>   That's my own opinion, and the reason I say that is
> because about 95 per cent of documents that are classi-
> fied ought not to be.
> Q. Mr. Anderson, is there any provision in law by regulation
> for such a study by a committee or newspapermen?
> A. Oh, I was giving my opinion.

Q. Yes.

A. I don't know of any such thing.

Q. Whether you are right or wrong in that, there is no such practice or procedure now, is there?

A. Not that I know about.

Q. Who does study them and classify them?

A. As I understand the procedure, it depends on the individual second lieutenant or first lieutenant or captain who happens to be looking at the piece of paper.

Q. It is a fair statement, Mr. Anderson, that your —

MR. DONOVAN: Just a moment.

MR. ROBB: Pardon me.

MR. DONOVAN: There is no testimony in the record saying that he has a source or sources —

MR. ROBB: I thought Mr. Anderson testified that he did have sources in these various departments.

By Mr. Robb:

Q. Didn't you so testify, Mr. Anderson?

A. I testified we have got sources all over Washington.

Q. Yes.

A. I don't remember going into specific departments.

Q. Do you have a source in the AEC?

A. Well, we have sources.

I think the answer to your original question is that any time any source of mine will agree to it, and the court will order it, certainly, I'll reveal the name.

Q. You make that contingent upon two things — (1) an order of the court and (2) your source agreeing to it; is that right?

A. Yes.

Q. Do you now have a source in the AEC?

A. Well, I'll give you the same answer.

Q. By "source" I don't mean the regular Public Information Officer, I mean —

Drew has been around Washington a very long time and there are those who have developed a certain tolerance for him. One cannot say the same for Jack Anderson. Observers in the Nation's Capitol do not see him in white, or even grey. Restraints which Drew on occasion has exhibited seem non-existent for Jack Anderson.

For instance, Jack saw nothing unethical, or even incongruous, in occupying the same office — Number 506 at 1612 K Street, N.W. — with a registered foreign agent, Irving Davidson. Davidson represented Indonesia, Nicaragua, Ecuador and Haiti. It was Davidson who finally asserted he was "feeling the heat" and who moved out to another office in the building.

Yet Anderson helped create a major national scandal over a Senator having much less intimate relations with another American public relations man registered as a foreign agent.

Is this moral? Is it ethical?

Many in the Washington Press Corps who watched the Pearson column become more unrestrained after Bob Allen went off to war, are now asking: When Jack Anderson takes over, will the lid blow entirely off, scattering fire and brimstone everywhere? Whatever the answer, a little cloud no bigger than a hammer-and-sickle hangs over the future of The Merry-Go-Round.

Soviet Roulette

One of the many puzzles in the Drew Pearson story is his relations with Soviet Russia and to Communism. During the nearly 40 years which have passed since Stalin's first "Five-Year Plan," Drew has achieved a growing personal acceptance in official Soviet circles and is frequently quoted by Russian leaders in support of their anti-American policies. He has frequently been aligned with the communists on domestic issues and some of his leg-men have had communist affiliations. Has he done this to create a sensation? What has been his motive?

Drew once suggested that balloons be launched over the Iron Curtain in order to get word to the Russian people in spite of their communist leaders' jamming of the air waves and their refusal to allow American publications on their news stands. He has also on occasion jabbed at the communists.

Yet as late as September 2, 1966, Pearson wrote in his column:

"In Cairo in May, 1964, I talked with Khrushchev. He gave me a message for President Johnson regarding cooperation between the United States and Russia over Cuba."

In these off-hand words, Pearson disclosed that he had been willing to act as a go-between for the then Soviet Premier in connection with an island right off our coast which was then, and still is, a Soviet base. Despite a strong inclination to do so, it is thus difficult to avoid the subject of communism in any honest work on Drew Pearson.

For instance, Alger Hiss, then a ranking State Department official, slipped Drew Pearson the British anti-communist guerrilla Order of Battle in Greece, and Pearson published it.

General Douglas MacArthur raged when someone in Washington slipped Pearson MacArthur's troop dispositions in Korea and Pearson published them.

Harry S. Truman, as a new President, was being tough with the Russians and Molotov was, consequently, threatening to wreck the United Nations organizing meeting in San Francisco. Pearson immediately wrote that Truman could not get along with the Russians as well as the recently deceased Franklin D. Roosevelt. Truman wilted, and even began to talk of Soviet Dictator Stalin as "Good old Uncle Joe."

Drew is still at it.

"In Moscow in the winter of 1965," he wrote recently, "I found Soviet leaders indignant over the new Johnson policy of bombing North Vietnam."

Then ignoring the fact that the Soviet Union is many hundreds of miles from North Vietnam and is arming the Vietcong with everything from machine-guns, mortars and MIG-21s to fight

American forces, Pearson declared: "To bomb
North Vietnam just after Kosygin arrived, the
Russians told me, was comparable to Russia
bombing Mexico just after the President of the
United States arrived in Mexico City for an of-
ficial visit."

Mexico, of course, is our next-door neighbor
and we are not arming her to fight Soviet troops.

In nothing else, the record shows, has Drew
Pearson been so consistent as in his attitude toward Russian communism. Drew, for instance, has
attacked every chairman of the House Committee
on Un-American Activities, beginning with Republican Hamilton Fish of New York and Democrat
Martin Dies of Texas. Pearson's exposure sent
one Chairman, Parnell Thomas, to jail for padding
his payroll. Then Pearson went after his successor,
Chairman John Wood of Georgia, again questioning his financial integrity, although this time in
vain.

"It was Pearson who first broke the inside
story (about Wood)," crowed the *People's World*,
an official communist publication. And it justified
the action thus:

"Pearson emphasized that Wood was the ranking
Democratic member of the Un-American Committee while Thomas headed it." And this was
"when Eugene Dennis, Communist Party general-
secretary, was held in contempt and imprisoned."

Wood, the publication made clear, deserved at
least the same; Pearson himself claimed directly
that his charge against John Wood, which proved
abortive, involved "a penitentiary offense."

Pearson attacked the careful Richard M. Nixon,
who is credited with the questioning that exposed
Alger Hiss as a Soviet agent. Drew went after

Nixon incessantly for years and is widely credited with being one of those who cut him down in the 1960 election. Drew went after Senator Joe McCarthy and helped pursue the Wisconsin Senator to his censure by the Senate and his early death. Anti-communists have been, and are, Pearson's meat: Senator Tom Dodd and General Julius Klein merely being two of his latest targets.

While he was among the first-line in the media attack on Joe McCarthy, it must have piqued Pearson that it was columnist Doris Fleeson, and not he, who coined the phrase "McCarthyism" and James B. "Scotty" Reston of *The New York Times* who made the epithet, "McCarthyism," respectable. It probably touched him in a tenderer spot that a conservative Republican — John Bricker of Ohio — was responsible for the *bon mot* on Senator Joe. Long before McCarthy's censure by the Senate, the Wisconsin solon entered the Republican cloak room at the Capitol and told assembled colleagues that he had been hunting near his home and had shot a deer. At this point Bricker laid down his newspaper, removed his spectacles and, looking searchingly at Joe McCarthy, remarked: "With a shotgun, I presume."

Joe McCarthy, moreover, had jumped in first, with his usual impetuousity, and announced that Drew was guilty of "complicity" with communism. McCarthy then added injury to insult by punching Drew Pearson in the men's room of the fashionable Sulgrave Club with, of all people, Dick Nixon stepping between them to prevent a further brawl.

Pearson hasn't been as lucky with anti-communist Irishmen as with others. Washington attorney Patrick Clark slugged Drew in another men's room, this time in the Mayflower Hotel,

for what Pearson had written about him. Clark
had been highly successful in getting money out
of Congress for Spain. Again others dragged the
battlers apart. Drew claimed he did all right,
but the Press Corps consensus was that the
battling Quaker is more successful with words
than fists.

Pearson, however, has not confined himself to
writing and speaking where communism is involved. The *Daily Worker,* official organ of the
Communist Party, USA, reported June 26, 1947,
that Pearson testified in Federal Court for the
District of Columbia on behalf of the 16 leaders
of a "Joint Anti-Fascist Refugee Committee" on
trial "for contempt and conspiracy."

"Drew Pearson," stated the *Daily Worker,* "appeared in Court to testify to the undemocratic
character of the House Un-American Activities
Committee."

Now to this day it has not been possible to
muster more than a handful of votes out of 435
plus in the House, among the elected representatives of the American people, against the House
Committee on Un-American Activities. The only
conclusion that appears logical is that it is undemocratic to disagree with Drew, who has recently publicly announced that he is the "conscience" of Congress. It should be added that it
was the House as a whole which voted the contempt citation for the 16 leaders of the Joint Anti-
Fascist Refugee Committee.

The Washington Press veterans have privately
and publicly long debated the reasons for Drew
Pearson's activities which, when the cards were
down, so frequently ended up defending communist
interests.

Declared Cissy Patterson's *Washington Times-Herald*, August 11, 1946: "When Hitler rose to power in Europe, a collection of un-American crackpots, intellectuals, intrigue lovers, revolutionaries and plain crooks saw an opportunity to get rich over here and at the same time to build up their apparent importance."

"Pearson is just one example, but he worked out of Washington and we know him." With Pearson, the *Times-Herald* went on, "apology and special pleading for communist Russia" constituted "an old line which he has been peddling without variation from the day the United States recognized the Soviet regime in 1933."

"Many people were taken in and believed the guff to the effect that Russia was our great ally and had gone to war to save us," continued the *Times-Herald*. "No mention was made of the now forgotten fact that Hitler and Stalin jointly pulled the trigger that started World War II in 1939 — and nobody in Russia ever lifted a finger contrariwise until Hitler attacked Russia in 1941."

It was amidst the war-time ally atmosphere cited, when ordinary people believed that real peace would follow the end of World War II, that Pearson helped change a newly tough U.S. policy toward Soviet aggression by charging that President Truman did not get along with the Russians as well as did FDR. It was not, in fact, until several years later, after the Russian communists took over Czechoslovakia, that Winston Churchill at Fulton, Missouri, publicly branded Soviet Russia a menace to world freedom in his famous "Iron Curtain" speech.

But leaving his domestic detractors and critics

aside, Drew Pearson has been perhaps the most quoted American by the Soviets in their own propaganda broadcasts to their people and to the world. Drew, in fact, has the highly unusual distinction of being the only American media man ever quoted by a Soviet leader in an "election" speech and that in Moscow itself.

Beginning a speech "Dear comrades" at an "election" meeting February 27, 1963, Nikita Khrushchev ridiculed American campaign promises saying:

Various promises of golden mountains and rivers of milk are made. What do you expect? This is sales talk of which there is plenty I should say, according to tales about this in the West. One of them goes something like this. A candidate of one party was making an election speech and called on people to vote for him. If our party wins the election, he told the voters in a certain village, we shall build you a new bridge. But there is no river here, why should we want a bridge? The voters asked in bewilderment. Never mind that, the candidate replied, we will bring you a river as well. (Laughter)

Then Khrushchev followed by quoting Pearson as follows:

An interesting judgment of the current situation in U.S. democracy is contained in an article by the well-known American Journalist, Pearson: "Many people will write today about Lincoln and the aims he advanced — the rule of the people, by the people and for the people. They will also meditate on how many people can be deceived, and for how long. The situation has not changed very much since the time of Lincoln. In a dictatorship it is necessary to keep the people in a quiet state. In a democracy — the American journalist has in mind democracy in the United States — it is necessary to fool at least 51 per cent of the people all the time, or to fool all the people for 51 per cent of the time."

And further the journalist writes: "If Lincoln were alive today and in an ironic mood, he might paraphrase one of the lines of his message thus: The rule of the rich is by the will of the rich and for the rich." This is true. This is really well said, truthfully said.

In the same article it says that tens of millions of Americans live in poverty.

Now even critical journalists may have an interview with the Soviet ruler of the moment if it serves communist purposes. The journalistic ore produced may be newsworthy, as William R. Hearst, Jr., and his "team" found. Pearson, however, seemed able to get together with Khrushchev almost at will. One of his columns, datelined Gagra, Georgia, USSR, as published in the Raleigh *News & Observer* of August 22, 1963, began "The last time I interviewed Khrushchev" and then, much later, Drew was able to get right to the carefully guarded Soviet Boss at the Aswan dam in Egypt.

In 1963, Drew Pearson took Chief Justice Earl Warren of the Supreme Court with him to meet the Soviet Prime Minister. Drew reported Agnes Meyer as participating in his "interview" but did not, in a series of articles, mention Chief Justice Warren, whose meetings with the ruler of communist Russia were thus carefully guarded as a secret.

Pearson, for his part, reported on this interview that "Socialist Life Keeps Khrushchev Young," according to the headlines on his column in the Washington *Post* of August 24, 1963.

"When I asked how he kept so young," reported Pearson, Khrushchev replied: 'It is the good Socialist life I lead."

Immediately thereafter in Bucharest in a Pearson column dated September 3, Drew said he talked with Rumania's Communist Boss, Gheorghiu-Dej, and reported: "Rumania in the old days was the most graft-ridden country in the Balkans.*** Gheorghiu-Dej is certainly right that Rumania is making progress because it was so far behind."

In a dispatch run August 30, also right after he had seen Khrushchev, Drew reported an interview with Soviet Ruler Todor Zhivkov of Bulgaria during which a tea was served. This consisted of "caviar, two kinds of sausage, two of cheese, nuts, ice cream, cake and coffee." While munching this proletarian fare, the Bulgarian ruler was able to tell Pearson that Khrushchev hadn't meant it when he said he would "bury" us and to assert atomic war will destroy Bulgaria "so we hope relations between us will improve."

And from the first non-communist country visited on his trip, Turkey, Pearson declared flatly in his column on September 6, 1963:

"The tough, unrelenting communism of Stalin's day is past, replaced by liberal Socialism and even a certain amount of free enterprise." This was less than a year after the Cuban missile crisis and while Soviet and satellite secret police were operating right off our coast in Cuba, controlling by murderous terror those Cubans who had not fled their native land.

While the Cuban missile crisis was building to a climax, it was former Senator Kenneth Keating of New York, now a judge, who called the shots on the Soviet missile build-up. Yet afterwards, in the winter of 1963, Radio Moscow Domestic "news" service told the Russian people:

"The fuss over Cuba*** has perfectly well-defined political motives. The usually well-informed U.S. observer Drew Pearson writes that when Senator Keating makes his war-mongering speeches about Cuba, thus reminding his colleagues in the Senate of the times of the late Senator McCarthy, we hear the voice of Keating, but it is Rockefeller who is doing the prompting.

"Pearson reports that Nelson Rockefeller is the chief Republican pretender to the Presidency of the United States in the next election."

Also in 1963, in connection with his Khrushchev visit, Pearson wrote in his column:

"Castro (and therefore communism) is not the real trouble for the United States in Latin America." The trouble, according to Drew, was that "there is no middle class."

The Cuban official radio quoted Drew with great joy and great length on this. Earlier in 1960, Sergio Diaz Brull, an arrested Castro agent, asserted to U.S. interrogators that Drew Pearson and Jack Anderson were friends of his and were highly regarded for their "friendship" with Castro.

After Lyndon Johnson had landed the U.S. Marines in the Dominican Republic, next to Castro Cuba, Red China's international broadcasting service said from Peking on May 15, 1965:

"U.S. columnist Drew Pearson wrote that one reason the landing of Marines in the Dominican Republic has so riled some of our staunch friends in Latin America is because it comes on top of a long and consistent U.S. policy of supporting military dictators."

Woodrow Wilson, who tried to encourage democracy in Latin America by refusing to recognize dictatorial regimes, and FDR, with his Good Neighbor policy, must have turned over in their graves at this latter statement.

Then Pearson reported in his column April 26, 1966, that communist-supported Juan Bosch "will almost certainly repeat, or top, his 1962 election victory." He lambasted Joaquin Balaguer "Trujillo's loyal servitor for 25 years" whose "background makes it next to impossible" for him to win the election. He couldn't have been more incorrect. Balaguer not only won in free elections, but won overwhelmingly. But not before Pearson, by his persistent attacks, had added the scalp of Deputy Under Secretary of State Thomas Mann of Laredo, Texas, to his collection. Mann was blamed for advising the landing of Marines in what, as a result of the election returns, turned out to be LBJ's one outstanding international success.

Apart from being frequently quoted on Russia's and Red China's radio, on December 27, 1950, during the Korean war, Drew Pearson received an accolade from the U.S. communist paper The *Daily Worker* when it linked him editorially with the "Hollywood Ten," Paul Robeson, and others of the ilk who were alleged to have been "victims" of U.S. anti-communist forces.

This same day, coincidentally, the *Daily Worker* objected to American troops fighting the invasion of South Korea asserting:

"Let's leave Korea to the Koreans. Let us seat People's China in the UN and quit Formosa. We have no business in these territories of other countries. There is not a single reason why a single American boy should die attempting to seize or hold them.***"

A decade passed and a similar event occurred, the Soviet-supported invasion of South Vietnam. On February 17, 1966, Radio Moscow on an international broadcast declared:

"Well-known commentator Drew Pearson ridicules official claims that U.S. troops are in South Vietnam at the request of the Saigon Government to defend freedom and remarks: 'This is pure nonsense. Governments in South Vietnam follow each other in such quick succession that no one

can keep track of whether Big Minh, Little Minh
or simply Minimouse is in power."

And on May 21, 1966, Radio Moscow in its Eng-
lish language broadcast told the world:

"Well-known U.S. columnist Drew Pearson ex-
poses Lodge's role in the DaNang operation. In an
article entitled 'Lodge's Advice to Ky', published
in the *New York Post*, Drew Pearson says: 'The
inside fact about Premier Ky's dispatch of troops
to DaNang to crush his political opposition was
that U.S. Ambassador Henry Lodge advised him to
do it.'"

Korea or Vietnam. It would seem the place
changes, but the words and music are the same.
It was over LBJ's actions to counter communist
invasion of South Vietnam and the Dominican Republic that Drew Pearson and Jack Anderson swung
away from Lyndon Johnson.

On May 26, 1966, after moving far into the camp
of the Kennedys, Drew was still using the guise of
an intimate knowledge of Lyndon Johnson's ideas
to make some points.

"The United States," claimed his column, "is
ready to revise its long-time policy of barring
Communist China from the United Nations.*** The
President has learned the hard way that the key to
Southeast Asia is Red China."

But then, when almost at once, the Red Chinese
demonstrated violently before the Soviet Russian
Embassy and its satellite embassies in Peking,
Drew's tune immediately changed. He advocated
that Soviet Russia and the United States get together to deal with the Red Chinese.

"It will be difficult," Drew remarked, "to pick
up the pieces broken by the bombing, escalation
and Mr. Johnson's own vituperative vocabulary to

justify the war in Vietnam."

Nevertheless, Drew claimed, "with the Russian fear of Chinese communism still rampant," there was some hope the Kremlin and the White House could get together against Red China.

Where did Drew first get this theme? Right from the horse's mouth -- from Khrushchev himself in Drew's interview in August, 1963.

Khrushchev, as then reported by Drew, declared:

"I should say the Chinese people want peace. But, of course, better relations between the United States and the USSR will better stabilize the world situation."

Drew added that, in any such alliance of the USA and USSR against Red China, the Russians wanted to take the lead with China.

Drew said: "But I asked Khrushchev, wasn't one of the quarrels between China and the Soviet the fact that China did not believe in co-existence?"

"The Soviet Premier replied: 'Let us agree on one thing. Put the responsibility for negotiating with China on our shoulders.'"

Another question is why Drew Pearson, who is no one's fool, has had identified communists working for him. These include David Karr and Karr's wife, Madeleine. Both wrote for the *Daily Worker* on occasion. The Executive Director and Chief Examiner of the Civil Service Commission asserted Karr was an active communist. Harold Rushmore, once an editor of the *Daily Worker*, said, "I used to give him assignments. He, at the time, was working on one of New York's non-communist papers, and he had to show his communist card to get these assignments."

Senator Joseph McCarthy charged that David Karr "is the link between Pearson and the Communist Party." Adolph A. Berle, now a leader in the New York Liberal Party but then Assistant Secretary of State, testified before the Senate Internal Security Sub-Committee that Karr conveyed confidential information to Pearson.

There is no evidence that Pearson and Karr have ever broken; Karr has gone on to make a great deal of money. He left Drew's staff to join the New York advertising firm which handled the account of Lee Hats, then Drew's radio sponsors, and went on to become president for a time of Fairbanks-Whitney Corporation, formerly the Penn-Texas Corporation.

Pearson defended Karr against the attacks of Martin Dies, the first to expose him. In a speech on the House floor February 1, 1943, Dies stated:

"For two years Karr was on the staff of the Communist Party's official newspaper, the *Daily Worker*. There is not the slightest doubt that all members of the *Daily Worker* staff were required to be members of the Communist Party."

Over twenty years later, July 7, 1964, Drew wrote:

"It was over half a dozen years ago that David Karr sought out a Russian refugee in Israel named Alexander Zarkin and signed a contract with him for the Israeli Government and the Fairbanks-Whitney Corporation, of which Karr was then president, to pioneer a desalination process in arid Israel.

"Fairbanks-Whitney directors, irked at Karr because he spent money which did not bring immediate dividends, eased him out."

"But," applauded Drew, "this was the first private, commercial project of its kind ever built."

The one thing clear from this report is that

David Karr is probably the smartest of the communists, including Andrew Older, whom Drew ever employed and, second, that Drew had been in touch with Karr for decades after he left Pearson's employ. This is particularly interesting in the light of other facts.

Among the ideas advanced by veteran members of the Washington Press Corps for Drew's consistency on communism are these:

1. Drew needs a "social" compensation for the earthy contents of most of his columns, contents which the Alaska Supreme Court has recently held can be called "garbage."

2. The Washington *Times-Herald* cited "a desire to get rich" and charged that, moreover, "it satisfied his natural and overpowering lust for lying, smearing, intrigue, character assassination and spying, all of which, next to money, are his aims in life."

Pearson himself has given some indications that the first point, involving his Quaker desire to promote peace, may provide at least a partial explanation. Drew once suggested, as noted, that, to reach the Soviet people, we should go over the Iron Curtain with propaganda balloons. The prevailing winds are West to East and Drew's idea may have had merit.

On December 28, 1962, commentator Vladimslov Kozyakov noted over Radio Moscow that "The Washington *Post* yesterday published an article by Drew Pearson entitled, 'The time for peace is right now.' The commentator asked why Washington did not take the initiative in this. The reason, perhaps, was that this was just after the Cuban Missile crisis and John F. Kennedy and his aides were still too shocked by the nearness of disaster. This, nevertheless, was the opening gun in the campaign which ended in the Test Ban Treaty in 1963.

Shortly after the Test Ban Treaty was signed; under the headline "Russia has kept its word under K," Pearson blandly asserted:

"My own conclusion, from careful examination of the record, is that the Soviet Union has been a tough negotiator but keeps its word when given."

This statement, printed August 31, 1963, kicked up a ferment in Congress and the news media. Lt. General John W. O'Daniel (Ret.) snapped, "Just whose side is Pearson on?"

At the time of Pearson's statement, the Soviet Union had broken 500 international agreements, including 50 of the 53 it had made with the United States.

Also, Pearson apparently forgot that President John F. Kennedy had told the American people and the world at large on TV that Khrushchev, and his envoy, Andrei Gromyko, had lied to him personally when they assured him that Russia was placing no "offensive weapons" on Cuba at the very time medium-range ballistic missiles with nuclear warheads were moving onto Cuban pads.

There is no denying that Drew's interviews with Soviet leaders and the controversies he has created as a result of his activities involving the issue of communism have added grist to the media mill from which he has taken pure gold.

Yet anyone who has observed Drew Pearson's operation rather intently for years becomes aware, as indeed the record as outlined here shows, that Drew Pearson is not always a free agent. There are indications that Pearson's troubles come when two or more opposed influences come to bear on him at the same time.

And it must be noted that Joe Barnes, wartime Deputy Director of the Office of War Information, was at that time, and has been since, a pal of Drew's. Barnes' attitude subjected him to such public criticism that he was eventually dropped as Editor of the *New York Herald Tribune*.

Under Joe Barnes at the Office of War Information as an assistant and later an associate, was the pro-communist David Karr. Karr was head of the OWI's Foreign Language Division and he came under suspicion after the American Ambassador to Hungary complained about him.

Testifying before a Congressional Committee under oath, Karr, head of the Foreign Language Division, admitted to knowing no foreign languages.

This is the official text:

Q. Are you a specialist in foreign languages?
A. No, sir.
Q. Do you speak any foreign language?
A. No, sir.
Q. Do you read any?
A. No, sir.

Maybe why Drew Pearson has written, talked and acted as he has with respect to communism is not important. Perhaps his motives are high.

The over-all record, however, shows that, whatever his reasons and motivation, Drew Pearson has written, spoken and acted in a way that has helped the communists in almost every key showdown. He has attacked, with many successes, a long list of men in public life who have exposed, or tried to expose, communist activities.

No one has charged Drew Pearson, ever, with being a communist himself, which makes the record of his activities what Churchill, in another context, called a mystery wrapped in a conundrum. No one has ever denied either that Drew Pearson is a most "unusual guy." To paraphrase John O'Donnell's favorite lines: he may waddle like a duck, quack like a duck, and associate with ducks, but he retains a clear and uncontested constitutional right to insist that he is a prothonotary warbler.

The Dodd Affair

Senator Tom Dodd of Connecticut, although a liberal on domestic issues, is the incarnation of everything Drew Pearson hates.

He is an anti-Communist; he is considered a "hawk" on Vietnam; a persistent supporter of "Lying Down" Lyndon Johnson in the Senate and Presidential races; he was a friend of Jim Forrestal. He had been a member of the staff of the F.B.I. and was second ranking member of the Judiciary Committee and head of its Internal Security Sub-committee, bane of Communists and as such wouldn't talk to Pearson. He is a Roman Catholic.

There are other reasons why Drew deemed it safe to attack Dodd: Dodd had attacked the Senate "Club" in a fiery indictment on the floor of that august body and they could not be expected to give him much help. Democratic National Chairman Bailey of Connecticut was known to be panting for Dodd's job and Drew was busy collecting information on Bailey to assure his cooperation. Finally, Drew calculated that the Administration dared not break with him until after the Bobby Baker scandal was really out of the way. He saw his opportunity and he took it: In less than seven months, Drew Pearson and his partner Jack Anderson wrote nearly 50 columns attacking Dodd, in a pyrotechnic performance unmatched since Victor Hugo attacked "Napoleon the Little" from a safe haven on the island of Jersey.

Like Peggy Ann of the Harding legend, the Dodd affair seems to have begun on a couch in the Senate Office Building. At least so insisted the wife of Mr. Dodd's principal assistant, Mr. James Boyd, when in the Presidential election of 1964 she approached Tom Dodd's former law partner, Judge Blumenfeld of Hartford, Conn., to complain that Mrs. Marjorie Carpenter — then Dodd's personal secretary — was very actively alienating the affections of her husband, James, who had abandoned her and their four children. Trying to keep the Boyd family together, the Senator dismissed the Mrs. Carpenter. He was more lenient with James Boyd, who had been with him for many years, and kept him on through that year's national campaign.

However, he was unable to keep Boyd at the same salary of some $23,000 a year and, apparently, rather than take a cut in salary, Mr. Boyd quit Mr. Dodd.

Jim Boyd and Miss Carpenter (her husband sued for divorce) then decided that the course of ethical conduct at this point suddenly required them to expose their employer's confidential documents to the public.

As Mr. Bill Buckley, the commentator, caustically commented, in order to expiate their consciences they did not go to the F.B.I. or the Department of Justice, or even Mr. Boyd's Con-

fessor, but told the story to Jack Anderson. Under
the express direction of this Mormon "missionary"
they stole such documents for duplication as Anderson instructed them, but not before carefully
examining the contents of all Dodd's files — over
a thousand of them. All in all, they copied documents and letters exchanged with constituents of
the Senator, copies of exchanges of correspondence with the President and the State Department,
photocopies of letters to and from other Senators.
They even took copies of Dodd's correspondence
with his own children. In this systematic burglary
they gradually associated six other employees, including Dodd's office manager, Michael O'Hare,
who also virtuously left Dodd after many years
because he did not get a salary raise he asked for
his girl friend, Terry Golden.

At one time during a debate at a forum at
which Anderson took part, he opened a conversation with Dodd in which he confessed that he had
arranged to have certain files of Dodd's come
into his possession but vowed he would burn them.
Why these employees cooperated with Anderson
is hard to understand unless it involves the same
inducement Drew gave to the Navy clerk who
turned over confidential files during the war. Of
course, in the case of the two girl friends, it
might have been simply a case of *cherchez la
femme,* but, whatever the excuse, this burglary
took place in the Senate Office Building in June
of 1965.

The identity of the burglars has been known
since late January, 1966. The F.B.I. has conducted a thorough investigation of the burglary
and submitted a report on it to the Department
of Justice. The burglars themselves have con-

fessed their deed in sworn testimony before a Senate Committee, and they have further confirmed that over the week-end of June 12-13 and over the following week-end they surreptitiously entered the Senator's office seven times for the purpose of removing documents. But although the facts about the burglary have been established beyond dispute, and although legal experts have offered the opinion that the burglars were guilty of violating a number of Federal and local statutes, nothing has been done to bring the burglars to justice.

Senator Dodd took the case to the Attorney-General but found that the Department of Justice, like its namesake, was blind. The Katzenbach excuse was that the Department did not want to take action on any matter which was before a Senate Committee.

That the Dodd affair started with an acknowledged theft is not the least intriguing aspect of the whole affair. Regardless of who initiated the duplication of Dodd's files, it is a fact that in using the pilfered contents the columnists unilaterally repealed the Constitutional guarantee against unlawful search and seizure of a citizen's papers, under the guise of a "citizen's arrest."

Because Dodd ranks next to Chairman Eastland on the Senate Internal Security Sub-Committee, no one knows whether highly classified documents were also copied, and made public. What happened to the list of hundreds of security risks made available under subpoena to Dodd's Sub-committee?

Tom Dodd himself was an unpretentious Democratic lawyer from Hartford, Connecticut. He had served as a prosecutor in the Nuremberg trials of the Nazi war-criminals. He had built up a solid Connecticut law-practice in a firm which specialized in insurance matters. He served in the House of Representatives before being elected to the Senate in 1958. He was a respected Irish Catholic layman, who was following the foot-steps of the late Senator Pat McCarran of Nevada, one of the few men in American public life who have opposed communism and escaped being smeared or smashed.

The first whiff of brimstone came on January 26, 1966, when Pearson and Anderson suddenly charged that Dodd's relations with Chicago public relations man General Julius Klein "skirted" the Foreign Agents Act. Three days later, the Klein angle was unveiled in the following column:

The intent of the Foreign Agents Registration Act is to give full publicity to anyone representing a foreign government and what they do. There is nothing illegal about acting as a foreign agent as long as the American people are informed of the fact.

Sen. Tom Dodd (D-Conn.) knew this because he once registered as an agent for the government of Guatemala between his service in the House of Representatives and the U.S. Senate. He knows therefore that when he gives speeches in the Senate ghost-written for him by Maj. Gen. Julius Klein, a $160,000 agent for West German interests, the public is entitled to know it.

Gen. Klein has called on Dodd repeatedly as an errand boy. Last year, for example, he asked Dodd to stir up trouble at the Justice Department for a competitor.

KLEIN-DODD PLOT

"I am enclosing," Klein wrote to Dodd, Feb. 12, 1965, "a photostatic copy of the Registration Statement filed by a disgruntled competitor, Edwin Hartrich of Duesseldorf, Germany.

"I wonder if you have now written to the Department of Justice inquiring why Hartrich was permitted to act as a foreign agent without registering until finally forced to do so in December, and whether any disciplinary action has been taken against him.

"I think this move would do a lot to clear up the matter and you were good enough to tell me that you would do it."

DODD TOUTS KLEIN

In 1961 and again in 1964, Dodd touted Klein for member-ship on the American Battle Monuments Commission. But each time the honor went to another.

Having missed the opportunity to serve his country in the matter of battle monuments, Klein sought an appointment in 1962 to the U.S. Advisory Commission on Information.

"I am sure you will want to add your endorsement," he wrote to Dodd on July 14. "But what is more important, couldn't you take this up personally with President Kennedy and with Lyndon Johnson so that we do not lose this oppor-tunity by default, as happened last time?"

When this appointment, too, passed him by, he wrote bit-terly to Dodd: "You know, Tom, friendship is a two-way street, I don't blame you for what happened, but what I am more disappointed in is that I didn't hear from you at all, either way."

Dodd replied testily: "I did what I said I would do, but I am sure you will understand that I cannot guarantee any performance."

Still sulking, Klein wrote back: "Tom, I never expected you to guarantee any performance . . . Anyhow, this is water over the dam."

KLEIN'S MILITARY RECORD

Even more important than battle monuments to Julius Klein was his military standing. He insists upon being ad-dressed as 'General,' his rank in the Illinois National Guard and he is proud of his World War II record as a commander of the 23d Quartermaster Truck Regiment.

But there was a blot, it developed, on his military career. As a young man, he had fibbed about his age. His army file gave his birth date as Sept. 5, 1895 — six years earlier than the true date.

This small untruth was allowed to stand until the Army sought to retire him from the reserves for being overage. Klein hastily requested that the record be corrected to show his birth date as Sept. 5, 1901.

He was shattered when the Army made the correction but accompanied it with a letter of reprimand. Dutifully, Dodd

intervened for him at the Pentagon, and the tarnish was removed from Klein's brass hat.

DODD'S SECRET LETTER

Far more shattering, however, was the Senate investigation in 1963-64 of Klein's activities as a foreign agent. When
his industrial clients began canceling their contracts, Klein
not only rushed over to West Germany but sent for Dodd to
come help him impress the clients.

Dodd readily agreed, but he had one misgiving.

"I have been thinking about this," he wrote to Klein in
Germany on Feb. 14, 1964, "and I believe that I might be
more successful with the people in Germany if I talk to them
alone. I don't think it is at all necessary for you to accompany
me, and there is a chance that it might be misunderstood.

"You know how anxious I am to help you, and it is for this
reason that I want to present your case in the best possible
light."

Later Dodd made a remarkable mission to Germany on
behalf of a registered foreign agent.

**From this account, you would never guess that
Julius Klein had served in our Army in two World
Wars, was in charge of some 10,000 troops in
World War II, was a former national commander
of the Jewish War Veterans, and that his West
German account was only part of an extensive,
long-established public relations business in
Chicago. Seemingly, Drew Pearson believes General Julius Klein to be some sort of sinister
foreign agent, but let us quote two other opinions
which read as follows:**

Dear General Klein:

. . . I recall so vividly your splendid and efficient service
in the Southwest Pacific area. Your devotion to duty and your
resourcefulness and courage earned you the esteem and admiration not only of your Commander-in-Chief but of all
those with whom you came in contact. Our long years of
friendship have only served to cement and fortify this feeling
on my part. . .

Most faithfully,

General Douglas MacArthur

And from the former President:

I join the national convention Jewish War Veterans in paying tribute to Brigadier General Julius Klein whose distinguished service merits the respect and honor of all Americans.

Dwight D. Eisenhower

Senator Fulbright's 1963 investigation of the "sugar lobby" had disturbed the West Germans, who did not understand what makes Fulbright fulminate and who concluded that his grilling of Julius Klein implied official U.S. disavowal of the General. Neither were the American readers reminded that the right of any citizen to petition Congress is guaranteed by the Constitution, and that — in view of Dodd's Nuremberg experience plus 20 years of friendship — Klein was fully justified in asking him to end the West German misunderstanding, and that Senator Dodd had a perfect right and even a duty to help undo the mischief done by Senator Fulbright, incidental to Dodd's own official mission to Bonn to interview a defected Communist assassin. In this connection, it might have been recalled that President Kennedy was shot by a Communist-trained gunman and that Dodd's mission to Bonn took place in the context of the world-wide struggle against Communist terrorism. Also, in view of the Nazi genocide of Europe's Jews, it would seem in accord with American public policy not to permit an able and respected Jewish-American businessman, Julius Klein, to be sideswiped by Senator Fulbright and blacklisted by Bonn. None of these considerations was mentioned in Pearson's "Merry-Go-Round."

By February 9, Pearson and Anderson admitted their possession of Dodd's files, by reporting: "From secret letters and memos which were supposed to have been destroyed, this column has now uncovered the startling story of how Senator Tom Dodd (D-Conn.) flew to Germany to make a pitch with West German leaders and industrialists not to cancel their $150,000-a-year contracts with Julius Klein Public Relations, Inc."

Over the next few weeks, the columnists had a field day with the Dodd papers. Pearson claimed Dodd had been given an Oldsmobile by a Connecticut contractor; United Aircraft had helped him commute between Washington and Hartford, including flying up his pet poodle; that Dodd had urged the appointment of International Latex's Abe N. Spanel as Ambassador to France; the Senate Foreign Relations Committee had debated throwing Dodd off the Committee; and so on. In this connection, Pearson did not tell how, for the first time in our history, a Congressional Committee had the power to remove one of its own members. In any case, the story was false.

Then, on March 14, Pearson's column raised the issue of Dodd's campaign funds and his use of testimonial dinners to finance his political career. This one went to the Senate Ethics Committee at Dodd's request along with a charge that Dodd received a $50,000 campaign contribution from Teamster Boss Jimmy Hoffa, not mentioning that this was a legal fee paid by Hoffa under Court order for services to his opponents in the Union.

A strange interlude followed, when Attorney-General Katzenbach ventured to question the columnists, who grimly reported: "Katzenbach said he had not investigated Dodd in connection with the alleged theft of the Otepka papers!" A week later, Pearson reported: "The F.B.I. has leaked out word that it intends to wind up its quickie probe of Tom Dodd (D-Conn.) and his unethical conduct by the week-end — with a white wash." The Pearson-Anderson column asserted the F.B.I. role constituted a "police state operation."

Pearson next spread the story to the West Coast, accusing two leading Californians, Mayor Sam Yorty of Los Angeles and former Mayor George Christopher of San Francisco, of "Doddism."

Dodd brought suit for libel in May and Pearson claimed it was an attempt to stop his disclosures, and Dodd's relations with the huge Connecticut insurance industry were questioned, as though a Nutmeg State Senator could ignore Connecticut's greatest source of "invisible" income.

By mid-June, Pearson was back on Julius Klein and rebuked Senator Jacob Javits of New York for speaking up in behalf of the badgered public relations expert. By the 20th of June, the columnist complained that Senator Dodd was receiving unusual privileges at the Senate Ethics Committee investigation.

"With two or three possible exceptions," Pearson ruled, "senators are honest." And a week later, he reported that the three Dodd office-employees, who had Xeroxed Dodds papers, James Boyd, Majorie Carpenter and Terry Golden, were having a hard time getting jobs. But by the end of the month, Pearson had become philosophical about it all and deadpan warned that "Senators Should Be Careful in Letters:"

There are three morals for Senators to learn from the Dodd investigation. They are:
Moral No. 1. Don't write letters just to make someone happy.
Moral No. 2. Don't sign letters carelessly that your assistant writes for you.
Moral No. 3. Don't be afraid to be ungrateful to a cam-

paign contributor. Just because he is generous during an election doesn't mean he can't get you into an awful lot of trouble.

The above morals are inspired by the raft of letters written by various Senators to Gen. Julius Klein, the Chicago public relations man and the West German agent.

Pearson was trying to explain away why many outstanding men had written friendly letters to Julius Klein, among them Vice President Hubert Humphrey, Sen. Abraham Ribicoff, and Senator Jacob Javits. Senator Dodd's doing so must be made different.

The only thing left was to suggest that, in future, all letters from a Senator to Klein should begin: "Dear Julius and Drew Pearson."

In fact, Pearson went right down the line against Dodd all through the record drought, the stock market slump, the zoom in living costs, the racial riots, the downfall of Sukarno, the elections in the Dominican Republic, and the Vietnam War. Even when Martin Luther King got hit by a rock in a Chicago freedom march, Drew Pearson wanted to know who was telling the truth in the Dodd case and charged that Dodd got triple expenses for a single airplane trip to California, not mentioning that Dodd's office staff made all travel arrangements.

When a mad sniper shot students on a Texas campus, Pearson charged that the Dodd Gun Bill could help the sales of Colt, Remington and Winchester arms factories in Connecticut. One of his most poignant complaints was that Dodd had taken time out to answer a Senate roll-call instead of staying in his office for a pre-trial interrogation by Drew Pearson and Jack Anderson. Pearson was like a race horse with blinders. He couldn't see any of the big stories; Dodd was the one and only real story for him:

DODD'S VOTING RECORD

When we insisted that Dodd's deposition proceed on schedule, his attorney petitioned the court to permit Dodd to testify in his own Senate office. It is customary for a pre-trial witness to testify in the office of opposing counsel. However, Dodd argued that he wanted to be near the Senate in order to answer important roll calls.

The court acceded to Dodd's request. During the first day of his deposition, counsel was able to cross-examine him for only about 70 minutes, since he was absent for 45 minutes on a quorum call.

This was interesting, first because a quorum call should not take more than five or ten minutes; second because the Senator suddenly displayed an unusual interest in voting.

Senators who serve on key committees with Dodd have long noted his remarkable absentee record.

A brief survey of forty-four "Merry-Go-Round" columns devoted to a single Senator during a period of major world upheavals indicates the political counterpoint Pearson can perform when his authority is challenged. They are also, from a journalistic point of view, evidence of misplaced emphasis. Even if Senator Dodd is guilty as charged, there were more urgent things going on in the world that would appear to call for a national columnist's occasional attention. Yet, as the "Republican" columnist Roscoe Drummond pointed out, Senator Dodd had not been found guilty of any impropriety, let alone any crime or misdemeanor. On August 17, 1964, Drummond wrote:

Take the two cases of Rep. Adam Clayton Powell of New York and Sen. Thomas J. Dodd of Connecticut. Here is a vivid and inexplicable example of how a double standard of moral judgment manifests itself in public and political life.

Here we have one member of Congress — Rep. Powell — who is a convicted law violator, guilty of slander, guilty of evading the sentence of the court for nearly two years, and guilty of contempt of court.

But there is virtually no public nor political condemnation of this man for his many offenses — for his law violation, for his spread of disrespect for the courts, for the harm he did to the elderly woman he slandered.

He is thus far unpunished by law and unpunished by public or congressional opinion. He seems to be held virtually blameless by his political peers.

And, in contrast, there is the other member of Congress— Sen. Dodd. He has been accused of no violation of law and he is convicted of no crime. He is charged with being too friendly with a lobbyist for whom he did some personal favors outside the Senate. He is charged with improprieties in handling funds raised at testimonial dinners.

In Sen. Dodd's case, though the charges are unproved and he has not been convicted by any kind of court, there has been wide condemnation and he has suffered severely at the hands of public and congressional opinion before the issues have been adjudged.

This is what I cite as a double standard of moral judgment. I can't explain it and if readers have any good explanations I'd be interested to have them.

Sen. Dodd has appeared day after day before a jury of his peers, the Senate Ethics Committee, which is investigating the allegations of unethical acts which have been brought against him.

But on Sen. Dodd it seems as though the verdict — and a very condemnatory one — had already been rendered by public and political opinion. There is head-shaking all over Capitol Hill. He is being dismissed as a "lame duck" whose political career is at its end. The wake has begun.

But there is no headshaking, no wake in progress, for Rep. Powell, suggesting that he has been hurt or harried by offenses which go beyond doubtful ethics. He has been tried for slander, convicted, sentenced — so far unsuccessfully — and he goes gaily on.

If Dodd's offenses justify a Senate investigation, Powell's offenses cry out for a House investigation. But there isn't a stir in that direction.

Another columnist to raise his voice in protest against "guilt by vituperation" was the conservative John Chamberlain. On August 26, 1966, he wrote in the *Washington Post* "A Last Word in d'Affaire Klein," calling attention to the fact that the General had been as much of a target as the Senator in Drew's journalistic jeremiad:

The case of Sen. Tom Dodd, Democrat of Connecticut, has apparently been put in mothballs by the senatorial investigating committee pending further research into the uses which the Senator put the campaign money raised by the contested testimonial dinners.

So we won't know much about the ins and outs of the Senator's accounting practices until some time in the fall. But if Dodd's reputation for financial probity is to be left dangling for a few more weeks or months, it should be said in the interim that the charges that he did anything reprehensible by befriending Gen. Julius Klein, public relations man for West German industrialists, have collapsed utterly.

Indeed, the whole weight of the evidence is that Dodd's trip to Germany, in the course of which he told former Chancellor Adenauer that Gen. Klein had been unfairly represented in the West German press because of the grilling he received before the Senate Foreign Relations Committee, was an attempt to rectify a blatant injustice.

The fact is that Klein, a patriot who served America in two world wars, had been victimized by a sort of liberal "McCarthyism." He had voluntarily submitted to an interrogation by Sen. Fulbright's Foreign Relations Committee when it was trying to discover whether agents of foreign interests were exercising nefarious influence on the development of U.S. foreign policy.

Nothing was turned up to show that Klein had done anything to harm America. Yet the very fact that he had been grilled by a senatorial committee led to slanted news stories in the West German press. Not being fully acquainted with the nature of an American congressional investigation, the West Germans apparently took Klein's appearance before Sen. Fulbright as evidence of some sort of guilt.

This sort of thing is an old story in the history of Senate investigations, in which the Senators get headlines that have a one-to-one relationship with the vigor, not to mention the ferocity, of their questioning. When Sen. McCarthy was zeroing in upon a supposed culprit, the liberals wrote long articles protesting that the victim should be permitted the rights of defense that are accorded to any common criminal in a court of law. But nobody took up for Gen. Klein when, as a result of the Senate questioning, he lost a $50,000-a-year account with a West German client.

That is, nobody spoke up for Klein except Tom Dodd. Gen. Klein was quite within his rights as a citizen to ask Dodd to undo some of the damage resulting from the Foreign Relations Committee interrogation. And Dodd, in taking time out during his trip to Germany to speak up in Klein's behalf, was doing what any friend should have done.

It is unfortunate that the question of Dodd's finances should be mixed up in the public mind with the Klein matter. There is no relation, organic or otherwise, between them. The fact is that Dodd acted like an honorable gentleman in trying to undo a wrong done to a friend. In my opinion he should have been more aggressive in defending himself. There was no necessity for trying to prove that the good word he spoke to Adenauer for Gen. Klein was subsidiary to the main business of a trip to Germany undertaken to interview a confessed Soviet assassin. Dodd, as Vice Chairman of the Senate Internal Security Subcommittee, had a perfect right to defend Klein against the imputation that he had somehow acted to undermine U.S. foreign policy.

For the most part, however, the Fourth Estate sat on their hands and speculated among themselves on why Pearson had H-bombed a Connecticut Senator and a Chicago public relations man. Some thought it could be his column was slipping and needed a shot in the arm. Others suspected that Senator Dodd had refused to give Drew the inside track at the Senate Internal Security Committee and had to be disciplined. One Washington newspaper wondered whether there was any connection between the anti-Dodd crusade and the New Year's 1966 Soviet orders to the American Communist Party to get rid of four men in our public life: C.I.A. Director Admiral Raborn, F.B.I. Director J. Edgar Hoover, House Speaker John McCormack, and Senator Tom Dodd of the Senate Internal Security · Committee. Another newspaper questioned whether Drew Pearson went after Dodd only because the Senator was an effective anti-Communist.

It did not occur to anyone that Julius Klein might

be as real a target of the "Merry-Go-Round's" campaign as Dodd, yet on April 22, 1966, General Klein wrote Drew Pearson a long letter which included the following passage:

You called me a "German agent." Have you forgotten that you tried to get the same assignment that you have for the German Illustrated QUICK magazine with *Der Spiegel?* Have you also forgotten that you arranged interviews with the late President Kennedy and Vice President Humphrey for which you were paid? These were not storied under your own by-line, but you used your influence to get Hagen, editor of QUICK, to see these important people. You were anxious to get the same deal with *Der Spiegel*, and you were even willing to give up QUICK if you could have *Spiegel* exclusively. Of course, you recall our conversation at the Mark Hopkins Hotel in San Francisco in 1964 when I introduced you to Mr. Schreiber, editor of *Der Spiegel*, who then visited you in your Washington home.

You must also have my correspondence with you on this, and I also have in my records a strong recommendation to *Der Spiegel* to make this deal with you. Unfortunately, the chief editor of *Der Spiegel* turned down the project as too costly for his Washington budget, otherwise *Der Spiegel* would be one of your clients today.

Apparently Drew's reputed fee of $2,500 per article was too rich for *Der Spiegel's* blood and Klein's failure to deliver this lucrative assignment exposed the General to possible Pearsonian reprisals. Another angle, of course, was the fact that General Klein is staunchly and outspokenly anti-Communist. To do so without raising an anti-semitic issue among American Jewry, which respected Klein, would seem to call for a unique adroitness in manipulating facts and quoting out of context. No one has ever accused Drew of lacking such ingenuity! Drew indicated Klein dealt with ex-Nazis. The fact that Drew Pearson knew otherwise is obvious from the following article which appeared March 17, 1966, in *The Sentinel*, the voice of Chicago Jewry for 55 years:

Confrontation of Pearson, Klein Adds Drama To Bond Inagural:

Principal speaker at the dinner was Drew Pearson. General Klein was seated at the dais along with the newly installed officers of the 1966 campaign. In introducing Klein, David Zysman, director of the Israel Bonds office, said:

"I am particularly pleased to have on the dais as an honored guest one of Israel's great friends and a supporter of our cause from the beginning, General Julius Klein. He was one of the men responsible for Israel's getting more than a billion dollars in German restitution payments made to the victims of the Nazi terror.

"He arranged the historical meeting between Chancellor Adenauer and Prime Minister Ben-Gurion in 1960 which paved the way not only for better understanding between the two countries, and which also led to additional help in the interest of Israel's security.

He further stated that "Julius Klein has rendered invaluable service to the Jewish people which fact is attested by letters from various leaders, including Ben-Gurion, who have expressed their appreciation to him, particularly with respect to his activities in the German reparations. Through the years he has been a loyal and devoted servant to our people.

"Drew Pearson, who recently again started a vendetta against Senator Dodd and General Klein sat near General Klein when these statements were made. As he left for Washington he passed Klein's seat, patted him on the shoulder and said, 'Good-bye, Julius.'"

Amid all these journalistic fireworks and verbal Molotov cocktails, one thing stood out like a longhorn steer in a herd of Jersey cows. The man who had it in his power to send Pearson and Anderson to jail for theft had his own Texas reasons for keeping on good terms with the two columnists. This was made public when President Johnson invited Mr. and Mrs. Drew Pearson to attend the State Dinner for West German Chancellor Ludwig Erhard and then pointedly omitted both Senator Dodd and General Klein from his guest-list, the very men who had been the most active promoters of close U.S. relations with West Germany for mutual defense.

But maybe Lyndon is only waiting. Few have criticized his sense of timing.

Pearson and LBJ

Next to sex, the most fascinating indoor sport in Washington is to watch the fast action between that wily Texas politican, Lyndon B. Johnson, and Drew Pearson, the hard-shell Pennsylvanian who invented the "new journalism." It may become even more amusing than adultery because a relationship which began with Drew clobbering LBJ unmercifully, at a time when it was hard for the Texan to hit back, then changed into a strange and unexpected stage of limitless admiration and is now finally reverting to the old familiar mayhem at a moment when, as President, LBJ seems to be holding all the cards.

There have been others who though they, too, were holding a pat hand, politicians who thought they had finally "got" Drew only to find he had invented some amazing trick, or developed some unexpected backing that saved him the way a runaway horse sometimes saved the old-fashioned medicine man from his "comeuppance."

It is no secret that LBJ is sensitive to the news media and that he has a compulsion to attain a consensus-whoever has to be silenced in the process. Lyndon, in a career stretching back to the early FDR days, when he worked in the office of Congressman Kleberg of Texas, has survived, like Drew, all manner of scandals and happenings that would have eliminated other men from the scene—and has come up smiling.

This, in their widely different, yet adjacent fields, the two men have in common. And both can get down in the gutter, bite and kick, and both can appear well-tailored and bland in a drawing room, the most imposing figures present. Both have repeatedly been nearly counted out only to get up off the floor and win. They are both at times unpredictable and deadly. Drew is now taking off again after Lyndon. What is going to happen next? Is Pearson, finally, going to be knocked out of the ring?

As a Senator, Lyndon Johnson always had been a target of Drew Pearson and Jack Anderson who kept referring to him as "the oil Senator" and they would take a casual swipe at him when the occasion arose. This may have been because they regarded the Texas solon as a poor news source since he preferred to do his talking with Jack Bell of the Associated Press and two or three other Senate "regulars" among reporters. This always has been sufficient reason for a Pearson attack.

The reason why is mere speculation, but there is no doubt that they stepped up their attack on LBJ immediately after he became Vice President and kept it up until he became President, suddenly, by John F. Kennedy's assassination. Since LBJ was walking on eggs during his Vice Presi-

dency, with Robert F. (Bobby) Kennedy particularly
virulent and out to get him, the Pearson attacks
not only hurt — they were dangerous.

Typical was the one contained in Drew's column
of January 8, 1961, just after the first "Kennedy
Congress" met. Pearson's version of an event was
as follows:

Johnson Acquires New Nickname
By Drew Pearson

The first Democratic Senate Caucus of 1961 turned out to
be one of the most acrimonious and important of the past
seven years — all of it behind closed doors.

It started full of sweetness and light. Nominating speeches
were glowing. New leaders were elected by acclamation.
Then Sen. Mike Mansfield (Mont.), the newly-elected Majority Leader, announced that he would like to ask the Caucus
to authorize Lyndon B. Johnson to preside over all caucuses.

There was stunned silence. But before the ensuing debate
was over, Johnson, who has won a lot of nicknames in the
past, had picked up a new one — "Have-your-cake-and-eat-
it-too Lyndon."

Many Senators, even though voting for Johnson in the end,
resented a move to continue his power in the Senate on top
of his promotion to the Vice Presidency. Sen. Albert Gore
(Tenn.) initiated the closed-door debate with expressions
of surprise, disbelief and a request that Mansfield withdraw
his suggestion.

Mansfield refused, calling his request an important matter
of policy and explaining that he himself wanted to participate
in the Caucus debate and could feel free to do so with the
Vice President presiding.

Gore insisted that there was nothing to prevent the Majority Leader from participating in the debate, even while
presiding over it. He added that the proposal to have Johnson
preside would be misinterpreted across the country as a
power grab and that it would be in stark violation of the
constitutional principle of separating the executive and legislative branches of the Government. But Mansfield was
adamant, insisting on immediate approval of his request.

Precedent?

Kindly Sen. Carl Hayden (Ariz.) stood up and a hush fell over the caucus. Hayden seldom speaks, but now he suggested that Alben Barkley, as Vice President, had presided over Democratic caucuses.

Sen. Clinton Anderson (N. M.) suggested that Hayden make sure of his facts, adding that the role he attributed to Barkley didn't square with his own recollection. Several other Senators supported Anderson and Sen. John Carroll (Colo.) asked that the minutes be checked. Senate Secretary Bobby Baker, however, could come up with no minutes of Barkley's day.

Carroll wanted to know if Harry Truman had served similarly, and that stopped further discussion of a precedent.

Finally, Mansfield recognized Sen. Wayne Morse (Ore.), who had been trying to get the floor. Morse said he would like to support the Majority Leader but that he felt the proposal was in clear violation of the separation of powers doctrine of the Constitution. Johnson, he pointed out, now belongs to the Executive branch of the Government. There is no place for him in Democratic cacuses, he said.

Morse went on to say that Johnson is now an advisor to the President, with whom the Caucus may find itself in disagreement on important issues. The right to disagree must be retained, Morse continued, and he sided with Gore's suggestion that the proposal would be misunderstood as a Johnson attempt to maintain his control over the Senate.

Mansfield Irked

Throughout it all, Vice President-elect Johnson sat in the presiding officer's chair — silent. Mansfield, however, began to lose his temper. He stated that he, not Johnson, would lead the Senate, and he added that he had discussed the matter with both Sen. George Smathers (Fla.) and Sen. Hubert Humphrey (Minn.) and that they were in agreement with him.

Meanwhile, Smathers had been whispering frantically to Sen. Richard Russell (Ga.) and the latter rose to support Johnson. Morse then demanded a roll call vote and assured the Caucus that he would vote against the proposal.

The harassed Mansfield argued that Johnson would have no vote in the Caucus, would simply answer questions. Sen. Olin Johnson (S. C.) drawled that he didn't think the Senate could get away with it. He pointed out that all future Vice

Presidents would have to be invited to preside and that under many circumstances this could be embarrassing.

Sen. John Pastore (R.I.) volunteered that he had been lieutenant governor of his state and had always presided at Democratic caucuses.

Sen. Philip Hart (Mich.), however, observed that some of those present had tried unsuccessfully to be governors — himself among them. He did get to be lieutenant governor, though, he added, and in the capacity was excluded from a Democratic caucus. He said he was disturbed about it at the time, but came later to realize that those who called him the eyes and ears of the governor were right in barring him.

Mansfield again refused to withdraw the proposal, this time at Anderson's suggestion. He assured the meeting that Johnson had not been consulted on the proposition beforehand. This evoked only skeptical Senate laughter. Johnson maintained his silence as he watched his party splinter over the issue of his future power in the Senate. But he made no move to withdraw either his name or himself.

Probably the strongest argument came from Sen. Mike Monroney (Okla.), who declared that the Senate was creating a precedent of concrete and steel. It was not only in violation of the principle of the separation of powers, he said, but the Senate would lose its power by having a representative of the Chief Executive watching its private caucuses.

No one, he said, could make a speech without realizing that it would be reported back to the President, and eventually the Senate would come under Executive domination.

At one point, Sen. Eugene McCarthy (Minn.) even remarked that what went on in the secret caucus probably would leak to the press and the whole story would be read in Drew Pearson's column.

Sen. Joseph Clark (Pa.) rose to change his vote in favor of Mansfield's proposal, explaining that the motion obviously would be passed. He urged for unity's sake that others follow suit. Sen. Paul Douglas (Ill.) said he was sorry to hear Clark switch his position and that he would continue to vote against it as a matter of conviction

Then came the one truth-revealing line for which Pearson critics have learned to watch in such "inside" reports.

"The final vote in favor of Mansfield and Johnson was 46-17," Pearson could not avoid reporting. But then, he explained it away in his usual airy fashion when on the spoor of a victim.

This overwhelmingly pro-Johnson vote, Drew casually explained, "did not represent the true sentiment of the Senators present, many of whom were embarrassed by Johnson's continued presence in the presiding chair."

An "under-current of resentment" also continued, Pearson held, "against Johnson's desire to have his Vice Presidential cake and eat his Senate cake."

Two days later, January 10, 1961, Pearson-Anderson were back at it again dragging up their version of details from the new Vice President's past and forgetting that Lyndon Johnson and House Speaker Sam Rayburn were close friends and associates until death claimed the latter.

Here is the bit which summarized some of their earlier statements against LBJ:

Anti-Johnson Senators Boiling
By Drew Pearson

Likable Lyndon Johnson, Vice President-elect, has done a lot of good things for his country. He has also done some things he would like to forget. During and since recent closed-door caucuses of Senate Democrats these forgotten events seem to be crowding back to other Senators' memories.

The meetings have scarcely been mentioned in the press. The public hardly knows they are going on. They are behind closed doors, and no minutes of the debates are taken.

However, this column can report that Senator after Senator has boiled against Johnson for trying to keep his power in the Senate as Democratic caucus chairman, after his election to the exalted position as Vice President. The comment has been acid.

"We should draw a line midway between the Senate and

the White House," remarked one Senator, "and erect a monument to Johnson standing, one foot on one side of the line, one foot on the other side."

"No," remarked another Senator, "since Johnson was chairman of the Space Committee we should float the monument by balloon, but anchor it one side toward the White House, one side toward the Senate."

A lot of things Senators had forgotten about Lyndon have come flooding back, and the more they talk, the more they remember.

Here are sone of them:

Unforgotten event No. 1 — Romance with Gov. Shivers — After Gov. Allen Shivers of Texas knifed Adlai Stevenson in 1952, Speaker Sam Rayburn vowed never to trust him again, refused to make peace with Shivers at a Texas breakfast arranged by Johnson to bring Shivers back into the good graces of Texas Congressmen.

In secret meeting after meeting Johnson romanced the Dixiecrat Governor, proposed all sorts of compromises. Mr. Sam meanwhile kept aloof. In the end Shivers kicked Johnson in the political teeth, bucked the Democrats again in 1956, raised money for Nixon, and tried to defeat both Kennedy and Johnson in 1960. Sam Rayburn was right, but he couldn't make his protege Lyndon see it.

Unforgotten event No. 2 — Sen. Joe McCarthy — On Jan. 1, 1953, a special Senate investigating committee headed by Sens. Carl Hayden of Arizona and Tom Hennings of Missouri brought in a shocking report on Joe McCarthy. They photo-stated the amazing bank accounts and deposit slips showing how McCarthy collected thousands of dollars supposedly to fight communism, used the money to speculate in the commodity market for his own personal gain.

It was one of the most devastating and conclusive reports ever made on a U. S. Senator.

Accordingly, some Senators, including Margaret Chase Smith of Maine, Flanders of Vermont, Fulbright of Arkansas, Ives of New York, Hennings and Hayden, wanted to ask McCarthy to stand aside and not take his Senate seat until all Senators had studied the record. They tried to get support from their new Senate leader, Lyndon Johnson. But their new Senate leader ran like a scared rabbit.

For two whole years Lyndon waited — during which McCarthy crucified people inside and outside Government,

during which he set the U. S. missile program back for
months by scaring key scientists out of Government. Finally
after Joe stubbed his toe in the Army-McCarthy hearings
and had lost popularity, Johnson moved in. By that time it
was easy.

Forgotten event No. 3 — the Natural Gas lobby — In 1956
Johnson masterminded a drive to pass a natural gas bill
giving his friends, the Texas gas and oil men, special
exemption from regulation by the Federal Power Commission. They had contributed heavily to his campaign. He made
no secret that he was out to help them.

His former assistant, John Connally, currently nominated
to be Secretary of the Navy, was chief lobbyist for the oil
gas companies. With Johnson's powerful pushing, Connally
did a masterful job. The gas bill passed.

But Elmer Patman, lobbyist for Superior Oil, with whom
Connally worked, financed a $2500 bribe offer to Sen. Fran-
cis Case of South Dakota. When Case revealed the offer
on the Senate floor, Connally sat white-faced in his hotel room
in the Mayflower all day. Though he masterminded the lobby,
he was never called as a witness in the investigation of the
gas lobby that followed. Lyndon abruptly removed the investigation from anti-gas Senators Hennings (Mo.) and Gore
(Tenn.), placed it in the hands of Arkansas' McClellan
whose law firm in Little Rock then represented Standard
Oil of N. J., Seaboard Oil, Tidewater Associated Oil, and
Carter Oil.

These are some of the forgotten events which come
crowding back to Senators' memories as they discuss the
rules of the Senate and the demand that Lyndon Johnson
continue to preside over Senate caucuses at the same time
he serves as Vice President of the United States.

After these and many similar stabs in the back,
Drew Pearson and Jack Anderson could have expected dire things, down to and including their
elimination as columnists, when, in one historic
second, Lyndon Johnson became President and the
man with all the weapons at his command to end
the careers of these two adventurers with words.
Aware of Lyndon's reputation for vindictiveness,

acquaintances say both men were openly quaking in their boots.

Yet suddenly in that late Fall of 1963, everything changed. For the first time since the war years of FDR, Pearson was one thousand per cent plus for a President. Lyndon Johnson was met, metamorphosed into a magnificent leader who could do no wrong. His enemies were Pearson's and Anderson's enemies and felt the bite of their flaying whips. Something obviously had happened. What?

One version has it that, with Johnson at first jibbing, mutual friends had brought them together after Drew agreed to and, subsequently did, eat crow.

It seemed, however, that, for once at least in his life, Drew was plain grateful.

Washington had been rocked in the early Thirties when Mrs. George Abell left the home of her husband and moved into Pearson's house in Georgetown — and even more excited when, shortly thereafter, she gave birth to a baby son.

When George Abell, scion of the family which owned the *Baltimore Sun,* sued for possession of the boy, Drew went into Federal Court in Washington and defended his right to custody of Tyler Abell so convincingly that later, when the child's legal father kidnapped the baby and took it to the Channel Islands, Scotland Yard compelled Abell to return little Tyler to Drew Pearson.

Lyndon Johnson now appointed the youngster, whom Drew had brought up, as Assistant to the Postmaster General and his wife was taken onto Lady Bird's staff. His enemies, of course, whispered that Drew was not just grateful but "bought off" by these appointments. Little did they know how dangerous Drew can become after he has apparently been taken into camp.

Whatever his motive, Pearson and Anderson heaped such lavish praise on LBJ that it was almost ludicrous in view of Drew's long carefully nurtured self-portrait of an observer willing to probe critically the actions of any official however high. He had sufficiently nettled one President so that he played a role in getting Drew fired from his news job, two Presidents had called him "liar" and yet another questioned his truthfulness more gently. So this sudden stickiness with regard to President Lyndon Johnson was more than strange; it was entirely out of character. Drew and Jack shovelled it on so thick that the most ambitious and uninhibited junior corporation executives would have been embarrassed to go so far. The two even surprised an already sickened Washington Press Corps.

By no word or public sign did LBJ indicate any appreciation of this cascade of favorable comment. For major leaks and reflections of his opinions he continued to use a handful of trusted press friends collected over a period of years, such as Jack Bell of AP or syndicated columnist William White. For hatchet work against those who really offended him, LBJ at least occasionally used Drew and Jack. In one case, Anderson was shown a Government dossier on a noted newsman. In this case, the worst Pearson could find to say was that he was "notorious."

However they had arrived with Lyndon, the Pearson duo were in a position Drew always sought through succeeding years and persons — someone with enough weight to stand behind him if he got in serious trouble — the kind of trouble that periodically assails those who reveal the contents of officially classified documents or who are participants in "bugging" private quarters.

Yet with Pearson and Anderson, in the very nature of their operations, no personal relationship in the official field lasts indefinitely; and usually not as long as this one — from the Fall of 1963 to LBJ's intervention to keep the Dominican Republic from going Communist.

For Pearson's progressive excommunication of LBJ, curiously, enough, began when Johnson sent the Marines into the Dominican Republic. Perhaps the politician with whom Drew Pearson has been personally closest in recent years is the Republican turned Democrat, Wayne Morse of Oregon. Pearson and Morse lunch often together in public these days, sometimes at the downtown Mayflower Hotel, sometimes on Capitol Hill. They are personally well-suited to each other. And, more important, they are in a position to be most useful to each other.

Senator Morse, chairman of the Senate Foreign Relations Committee sub-committee on Latin America, was, as one might expect, highly critical of LBJ's intervention in the affairs of an American Republic, even if this was to save American lives and to prevent a Communist take-over of the Dominican Republic. Pearson reflected Morse's views, although at this time in a more muted fashion.

Some say that Drew was angry, too, that LBJ did not make his step-son Attorney for the District of Columbia when the position opened. In fact, it was common gossip on Capitol Hill that you could tell which Senators were in Drew's pocket by simply noting those who were absent or refrained from voting on the confirmation of David Bress instead

of Tyler Abell for the post Tyler coveted of U.S.
Attorney for the District of Columbia.

The attacks of Senators Fulbright, Morse, Hart
of Michigan, Clark of Pennsylvania and other
"liberals" against LBJ's Vietnam war policies
probably, however, were the clincher in changing
Pearson's attitude toward Lyndon Johnson. Drew
has always attacked anyone fighting Communism
or warring against it. He was violently against
Harry Truman on Korea. He could hardly be expected to stay glued to LBJ on Vietnam.

Drew's and Jack's change of attitude on LBJ first
became fully evident in connection with their
"exposé" of Senator Thomas Dodd.

On April 23, 1966, their column declared:

> Lyndon is a friend of Dodd. It takes a real friend to make
> the two trips he made to Connecticut to speak at two testi-
> monial dinners which raised $100,000 for Tom's personal
> bank account.

In fact, without much apparent basis, Drew and
Jack made Lyndon the cause of the importance of
Senator Dodd. The Connecticut Solon had, after all,
served in the House for sometime after acting as
a prosecutor in the Nuremburg trial of Nazi war
criminals before moving into Lyndon's orbit in
the Senate.

The column continued:

> After the 1961 testimonial, Dodd's political lieutenant, Ed
> Sullivan, wrote to him: "Charles McDonough (an insurance
> executive) drove Vice President Johnson back to the airport
> from dinner. On the way, he told Charlie under no condition
> would he miss your dinner. He said he considers you and
> Grace (Mrs. Dodd) amongst the best friends of he and Mrs.
> Johnson, and considers you on the Senate floor the best
> friend he has."
> Lyndon did all right for Tom. He hoisted him to a choice
> position on the Senate Foreign Relations Committee, ahead

of other Senators, a vantage point from which he was able
to work more effectively with Gen. Julius Klein. And he
almost picked Tom to run with him for Vice President.

Such is part of the inside story of what goes on in Washington.

By July 5, 1966, Pearson's column accused
President Johnson of having "bowed" to the Joint
Chiefs of Staff in ordering the bombings of military targets in the Vietcong base area of North
Vietnam. In connection with this decision, the column asserted:

"State Department advisors pointed out that a
North Vietnamese delegation was enroute to Peking
to get more aid from the Red Chinese. Ho Chi
Minh was reported to be in the delegation. It was
argued that this was the worst time in the world
to start peppering Hanoi and Haiphong because it
would play into the hands of the North Vietnamese
and force Peking to give more aid.

"The first bombing of North Vietnam, February 7, 1966, started at the worst possible time
when President Kosygin of Russia was visiting in
Hanoi trying to persuade the North Vietnamese to
sit down at the peace table."

And by July 7, Pearson and Anderson were really letting the man who so recently could do no
wrong as far as they were concerned get it from
both barrels.

"The tragedy," they wrote, "is that the President is rapidly painting himself into a position
where the great things he has accomplished on the
domestic scene will be both forgotten and undermined.

"He is painting himself into a position where
the American people will conclude that the only
way they can get out of this war is to elect a new

President with new policies and do it as quickly as possible — in 1968.

Then — perhaps to assist Wayne Morse — Pearson attacked what has been widely praised as Johnson's outstanding success in foreign affairs:

> Every so often, the President's old habit of siding with the generals, and his latent Texas instinct for shooting from the hip got the better of him and he sank the nation in trouble.
>
> This was what happened in the Dominican Republic where in 30 minutes he made up his mind to undo our quarter-century old policy of non-intervention.
>
> That 30 minute snap decision to land the Marines cost around $110 million and alienated our best Latin-American friends. Despite elections, they are still suspicious.

When LBJ met in early August, 1966, with Prime Minister of Britain, Laborite Harold Wilson, Pearson wrote of LBJ's relations with domestic Labor, "The romance is now over."

As Pearson led into this attack, he tried to put words into LBJ's mouth and indicate that the President was for recognizing Red China. In this connection, Pearson stated:

> The Lyndon Johnson who is now President has come to realize what Lyndon Johnson as a Senator did not realize — namely that you can't ignore a nation of 700 million people, especially when it has nuclear weapons, and that the best way to deal with a nation of such size and potential strength is to talk to it, not ignore it.
>
> * * * *
>
> The President has learned the hard way that the key to peace in Southeast Asia is Red China. He knows he will never get North Vietnam to sit down at the conference table as long as the Chinese are opposed.

Drew's attacks on LBJ were by late August becoming more frequent and more violent. Did he and Jack Anderson feel they had enough protection from LBJ's wrath? Certainly he could not count on this from the Liberals on the Senate Foreign

Relations Committee; most Washington observers felt the two writers were too astute for that. Yet at a moment when action could still be brought for revealing the contents of classified documents in a period of real war, Pearson and Anderson seemed to have lost their pristine fear of Lyndon Johnson. It was perhaps natural that Washington, knowing their animosity toward each other, wondered if Drew had climbed aboard the band wagon of Lyndon's *bete noire*, Senator Robert F. Kennedy, who, despite his demurrers, is obviously a presidential hopeful.

In any case, by August 22, 1966, the Pearson column piled onto LBJ for not being able "to control his two daughters, one from going abroad with a battery of secret service men when other U.S. citizens were advised to stay at home; the other from having a grandiose wedding when American boys were fighting and dying in Southeast Asia."

Lyndon, reported Drew, has been "an ordinary American-type father, no better than the rest of us."

"He's been like I am," said Drew, who induced his own daughter to turn over her Virginia farm to him as soon as she was of age, "a push-over for daughters."

"Like the rest of us, he has abdicated authority, and no family without an active, interested strong father produces considerate children."

From this point, Pearson-Anderson blamed the President for paternal faults which had caused juvenile delinquency, our racial troubles and "the unfortunate truth that the Beatles are more popular than Christianity."

Pearson and Anderson stated in print:

Old Joe Kennedy, patriarch of the Kennedy clan, would no more have let his son or daughter go to Europe at the wrong time or get married in an ostentatious manner at the wrong moment than he would have thumbed his nose at the Pope.

Let's face it, the Johnson girls did not show consideration for the fact that their father had been urging every other American not to travel abroad; and that he did not want his younger daughter to get married in the first place; and wanted her to do it as modestly and inconspicuously as possible in the second place.

Instead, Lynda wandered all over Europe getting headlines at every stop, and spending the taxpayers' money through her Secret Service escort; while Luci staged a wedding in the most prominent Catholic church in the Nation's Capital, whereas she could have been married quietly at the Johnson ranch with cameras barred altogether.

LUCK TO PAT NUGENT

This column is going to get the entire Johnson family sore at me, plus my own family, plus various fathers from Maine to the Rio Grande.

So I might as well make Luci's friends a little madder by saying that I wish Pat an awful lot of luck. Married to a girl with a $600,000 trust fund, accustomed to getting what she wants from the President of the United States, he'll need it.

However, he has one big thing going for him, as he himself indicated when he was asked on television what it was he liked most about Luci and without referring to her looks, her disposition or her charm, replied, "our religion." Fortunately the Catholic religion doesn't permit divorce.

The group of citizens that suffers most from deficient fatherhood is the Negroes — for a very good reason. All during the days of slavery, slave owners made it a practice to separate families. The strongest slaves were sold on the auction block, and this breaking down of the family, practiced for years, can't be repaired easily. It's one reason why some Negro men walk off from their families today, and why there is such need for Big Brothers and foster fathers among our Negro population.

Thus in rather characteristic fashion did Drew Pearson reciprocate for Lyndon Johnson's kindness to Drew's son and daughter-in-law. Highly significant was the fact that he pointed to the head of the Kennedy clan as a paragon of virtue and an example to youth. It meant that Pearson and his man Friday, Jack Anderson, were declaring open war on LBJ.

Their presumed calculation on Kennedy support seemed reasonable until you recalled that the Kennedy Clan, above all, are Catholics and know where Drew stands. Would even an ambitious Bobby or an amiable Teddy Kennedy expect a lasting deal with a columnist whose specialty had been headlong attacks on other Catholics — such as Mike Kirwan, Mike Feighan and Tom Dodd — and in the old days their own father, "Old Joe." He sneered at House Speaker John McCormack as "the archbishop of Washington," declaring it unsafe for the Speaker to be directly in the line of presidential succession.

Drew has repeatedly attacked New York's Cardinal Spellman, along with the Kennedy family, for the American involvement in Vietnam. The columnist is, in fact, the only man to accuse the Cardinal, who has visited our troops in Vietnam, of being a leading cause of what he calls "the Vietnam tragedy." In a column published on June 5, 1966, Pearson stated that the present war goes back to "three little-known events" one of which was "the intervention of Cardinal Spellman. . ." Apparently what Drew regarded as the Cardinal's poor judgement was Cardinal Spellman's wholehearted anti-communist position.

Moreover, it is doubtful that at this point the Kennedys are strategically placed to give Pearson and Anderson the highest level protection they may well need if LBJ belatedly accepts their challenge.

Lyndon Johnson finds himself in much the same position FDR did — he has Drew Pearson (and

Anderson) in a position where at any period LBJ's
Department of Justice, now firmly in LBJ control,
is in a position to begin prosecution of Drew and
Anderson unless they obediently play hatchet-man,
just as Drew, after the Navy files incident, had
to play FDR hatchet-man.

Although the Kennedy-Katzenbach Department
once pretended it must wait for the Senate Ethics
Committee to finish its inquiry before the Department could make a decision whether to prosecute
Anderson, and presumably Drew as an accomplice,
for the burglary of Senator Dodd's files, ultimately, LBJ's new Department of Justice will have to
face up to the issue. The Senators whom Drew
does not keep in his pocket will be pressing fiercely for such prosecution to protect the integrity
of the Senate's own files.

Then only LBJ can save Drew, who must rue the
day his partner pulled off a theft of Senate files in
which he himself announced the theft. If he can get
out of this one, Drew is a Houdini. It is a safe bet
that the politically shrewd LBJ knows the bind he
has Drew in and pressure will be applied as LBJ's
own reelection comes closer.

It was duly noted by the knowledgeable that LBJ
conspicuously invited Drew, enemy of West Germany and friend of Soviet Russia, to the Senate
Dinner for Erhardt, and conspicuously did not
invite Senator Dodd, the anti-Communist friend of
West Germany. Is this a cat-and-mouse game with
LBJ the smiling cat? And if so, whose was LBJ's
mouse, his old enemy Drew Pearson or his old
friend Senator Tom Dodd? The betting in the Press
Club on whether LBJ ultimately will dump Pearson
is not in Drew's favor.

The Brass Ring

In the period of "managed news" which began
with the censorship of World War II, there has
been a crying need for fearless, honest, outspoken
and accurate journalism. Drew Pearson has praised
himself for all these qualities and has taken the
line that if Drew Pearson had not existed, he would
have been created by necessity.

Yet the sad truth is that he has been anything but
true to his image. The record shows that, instead,
he has, in fact, served one master after another,
be it political or business or labor interest.

The years he has been operating have been characterized by the steady decline of the Press and
by the rise of radio and T.V. They have been
years of propaganda, pollsters and computers, of
"the right to lie" and other evidence of the decay
of free communication between human beings.
During such a period, the American people hun-
gered and thirsted for another Tom Paine, or a
Voltaire or a Ben Franklin. Instead, they got

Drew Pearson.

From the point of sheer endurance there is nothing to equal his performance: a total of well over seven million written words in the daily column plus hundreds of TV and radio scripts. He combined the crusading zeal of Joseph Pulitzer's old *New York World* with the industry of a Henry Ford, and then added the eavesdropping methods of Col. Mann's *Town Topics*. Drew Pearson's column is his own self-portrait. No man can possibly produce such an output over the years without revealing his own character and it was Drew's character, in the end, that undermined Drew's power.

That power was and is great. Whether you credit him with 400 papers and 60,000,000 readers or, 150 papers and perhaps as few as 10,000,000 potential readers, Pearson has power. By either calculation, he is in a position swiftly to present his views and his version of the facts to a large nation-wide reading public seven days a week, in addition to this he has his weekly radio broadcasts.

Moreover, as in the Dodd Case, he is quoted in the headlines and most top TV newscasts. In the general atmosphere of constraint and fear which stems from government by manufactured mass-opinion, few men in public life care, or dare, to challenge his authority. Now and then, Drew has tried to use his power constructively, as when he proposed sending balloons to drop propaganda leaflets over Soviet Russia or in his occasional friendly gestures towards world peace. The success of his "Friendship Train" after World War II suggested that his kind of influence could quite easily be exerted in a good cause.

That is because, if you take the position that the

end justifies the means, eventually the evil means corrupt the noble purpose which you pursue. An historical instance is provided by the Inquisition, which started from the premise that anything is justified to win souls for God: it swiftly progressed from preaching the Gospel to the burning of heretics at the stake. The moral erosion of Drew's Quaker conscience was inherent in the formula which he adopted to reach public success. What Jack Alexander, widely regarded as a distinguished reporter, once said in the *Saturday Evening Post*, is perhaps applicable today:

In so doing, he was hewing closely to a sure-fire formula for journalistic success. This formula began to come into its own with the advent of the political column which is syndicated, or sold, to large numbers of newspapers. It has reached its present full-blown development with the growth of the radio networks. Its success, on the radio side, stems from a passion for artificially contrived excitement which undeniably exists among large masses of listeners.

By working radio and newspaper syndication together, the exponent of the formula is able to wield a unique double-action influence on public opinion. The chief ingredient of the formula is aggressive indiscretion, and with it go various knacks for making and keeping enemies, preferably big ones; for making one's self, instead of the news, the focus of interest; for highjacking public controversies and creating one when none is boiling at the moment; for investing the most trivial items with a sense of urgency and drama, and, sometimes, for giving gossip the status of established fact. Because all this tends to build up the practitioner into a sort of journalist-politician, his product in print or on the air often takes on the punitive character of political prose of oratory. On the whole, the formula, when literally followed, bears as much resemblance to sober journalism as ax murder does to brain surgery.

This somewhat Lizzie Borden approach to the news has been responsible for some of Pearson's truly awesome performances on issues of fact and public personalities.

For example, it was understandable that Drew should have resented Senator Millard Tydings' insistence on the removal of his father, Dr. Paul Pearson, as Governor of the Virgin Islands. However, that does not explain why he falsely charged on a radio program in 1939 that Tydings had used WPA labor to build a road and a private yacht-basin on the Senator's estate at Havre de Grace, Maryland. When challenged Pearson airily explained that he hadn't even read the script before he went on the air and that "the whole thing was just a technical error."

So also, in November, 1943, Pearson broadcast a story about General Patton slapping a wounded G.I. private and thereby almost disrupted the Mediterranean command on the eve of the Anzio landing. Said Pearson: "I decided it was time to let loose on him (Patton)."

Another Pearson sideswipe was an election-eve broadcast in 1944, implying that Tom Dewey and John Bricker, the GOP national candidates, were draft-dodgers: an odd charge from a Quaker who had enlisted in the Swarthmore Student Army Corps five days before the Armistice in World War I.

Drew's famous "predictions" of things to come at one time scored as high as 60 per cent accuracy, partly by virtue of his breaking the Monday release dates on a Sunday night broadcast, but in two brief years they included some still exclusive forecasts:

He prophesied that FDR would not run for a fourth term in 1944 and that if he did he would be defeated by the Southern Democrats.

He predicted that Japan would stab Russia in the

back in the spring of 1943 and that the German end
of World War II would be over by September, 1944.

He also revealed that Robert S. Sherwood, Roosevelt's pet speech-writer, would be appointed U.S.
Minister to North Africa, and that Fala, the White
House Scottie, was about to become a father. One
was as wrong as the other.

During that time neither the crystal ball nor the
inside track seemed to be working for him in
many instances and they often don't now, but Drew
has a practice of calling attention when he guesses
right and forgets the rest.

The trouble seems to be that, having clad himself in the robe of Jeremiah, he's still wearing the
hat of a journalistic Jack the Ripper. He is con-
demned to keep on being called "an S.O.B." a sob-
riquet he himself repeats with great delight.

No other man in the long history of our free
press has actually caused his fellow-journalists to
consider the abandonment of political columns by
the nation's newspapers. This was reported on by
Jack Alexander in the *Saturday Evening Post*.
Alexander wrote:

Pearson sees himself as a gladiator for political rectitude
who would like to get away from it all. The pains of his
servitude, however, are mitigated to some extent by its financial rewards. He nets about $90,000 a year, before taxes,
from radio and his column alone. In view of these financial
rewards and his duty to humanity, Pearson is not likely to
retire to the farm. If, however, he should, a lot of people
would cheer, as he has publicly stated they would, and among
them would be a number of newspaper editors. Columns of
the shriller type, such as the Merry-Go-Round, have caused
much soul-searching in the past few years on the part of the
editors. Some have steadfastly opposed them, in spite of
their value as circulation getters, on the ground that they
overdo the sensational approach to the facts of life. Others
take the bread-and-butter view that the see-all-know-all

tone of the columns tends to relegate their own editorial pages to a position of secondary importance.

Next April, at the annual meeting of the American Society of Newspaper Editors, the question of whether to cut out the columns will come up for discussion. If this surgery is carried out, which seems highly improbable, it will be the first hysterectomy on record in which the patient has wielded the knife.

That was inscribed over 20 years ago and still the "Merry-Go-Round" goes around. And gosh! how the money rolls in. Truth still cries unheeded in the market-place, in danger of being sued for libel by Drew Pearson. Now aging and tiring, he can still lash out and crucify his victim. Even the Department of Justice still cringes and crawls before Pearson and also Jack Anderson, who has proved himself an apt successor.

Many years ago, Sir Wilmot Lewis of the *London Times* pointed out that the function of a free press was to comfort the afflicted and afflict the comfortable. Perhaps Pearson leaned a bit too heavily on the side of the afflicted, but he did provide a lot of entertainment to those who could not distinguish between fact and gossip. His column never lacked readers even if it did not always command respect; it invited attention and did not worry itself over whether the interest of its readers was sincere or simply scandalized.

With the power and influence which Drew's undeniable courage, ingenuity and persistence created, he could have become a real force for the good of our country and the peace of the world. His early conduct could then have been forgiven him, as many men are forgiven for what they did in their youth, provided their maturity justifies their career as a whole. Drew Pearson's very real strength has been earned by an almost incredible endurance-record.

According to Shakespeare, "It is excellent to have a giant's strength; but it is tyrannous to use it like a giant." Pearson has not used his strength like a giant but rather like a gnome, sometimes mischievously, sometimes maliciously, but rarely with magnanimity, humility, and almost never with restraint. Drew has accumulated a fortune but dug the grave of his reputation with his own typewriter.

In the early days of their column, Pearson and Allen would on occasion present to those who had earned their approval what they called the "Brass Ring." This was a reference to the old system by which riders on a merry-go-round snatched at a ring-holder as they went round and round. If the ring was nickel, you had to dismount at the end of the ride; if the ring was brass, you got an extra ride, free for nothing. It is a pity that in the case of Drew Pearson the ring should have been tinsel when the public expected gold.